W9-AJO-739

SALT ENCRUSTED BED OF LAKE EYRE

CORROBOREE ROCK OUTCROP IN PALM VALLEY

A FLOCK OF BUDGERIGARS AT AN OUTBACK WATERHOLE

SKELETAL BRANCHES IN A STONY, OR GIBBER, DESERT

FLOODED WOODLAND ON KIMBERLEY PLATEAU

LIFE NATURE LIBRARY
LIFE SCIENCE LIBRARY
GREAT AGES OF MAN
FOODS OF THE WORLD
TIME-LIFE LIBRARY OF ART
LIFE LIBRARY OF PHOTOGRAPHY
THE EMERGENCE OF MAN
THE OLD WEST
THE ART OF SEWING
THE GREAT CITIES

THE AUSTRALIAN OUTBACK

THE WORLD'S WILD PLACES/TIME-LIFE BOOKS/AMSTERDAM

BY IAN MOFFITT
AND THE EDITORS OF TIME-LIFE BOOKS

qQH
197
M57

E26674

ST. PAUL PUBLIC LIBRARY

© 1976 Time-Life International (Nederland) B.V.
All rights reserved.

THE WORLD'S WILD PLACES

European Editor: Dale Brown
Editorial Staff for *The Australian Outback*:
Deputy Editor: Windsor Chorlton
Picture Editor: Pamela Marke
Design Consultant: Louis Klein
Staff Writer:
Michael Brown
Art Director: Graham Davis
Designer: Joyce Mason
Picture Researchers:
Karin Pearce, Margrite Prah
Picture Assistants:
Cathy Doxat-Pratt, Christine Hinze
Editorial Assistant: Ellen Brush
Copy Staff: Julia West

Consultants
Botany: Christopher Grey-Wilson,
Phyllis Edwards
Geology: Dr. Peter Stubbs
Herpetology: David Ball
Ichthyology: Alwyne Wheeler
Meteorology: Lt. Cdr. Bruce Doxat-Pratt
Invertebrates: Michael Tweedie
Ornithology: Dan Freeman
Zoology: Dr. P. J. K. Burton

The captions and text of the picture essays were written by the staff of Time-Life Books.

Valuable assistance was given in the preparation of this volume by Time-Life correspondent: John Dunn, Melbourne.

Published by Time-Life International (Nederland) B.V.
Ottho Heldringstraat 5, Amsterdam 1018.

The Author: Ian Moffit, an Australian journalist, has written about many aspects of his native land and is the author of *The U-Jack Society*, a personalized view of modern Australia. In gathering the material for this volume he travelled thousands of miles by aeroplane through the Outback, visiting parts of central Australia that were unknown to white men less than a hundred years ago.

Special Consultants: Laurie Corbett spent ten years studying the ecology and social behaviour of dingoes in the Outback. As acting curator of fauna at the Arid Zone Research Institute in Alice Springs, he made numerous collecting expeditions in central Australia.

Andrew Kanis specializes in the botany of South-east Asia and Australia. He joined the Herbarium Australiense, Canberra, in 1969, and is currently Australian Botanical Liaison Officer at Kew, London.

The Cover: Bathed in early morning light, the domes of the Olgas rise from the desert plain in Australia's Northern Territory. In the foreground, a desert oak grows from the red Outback soil, which is dotted by spiky tufts of porcupine grass and the bleached trunks of drought-stricken desert poplars.

Contents

Arid Plains and Ancient Mountains

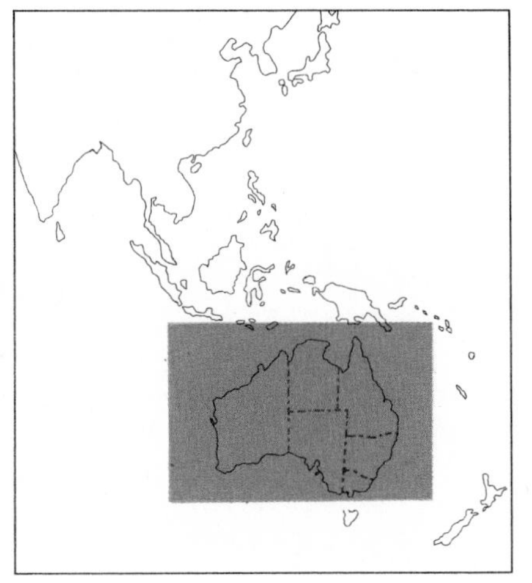

Australia, the remote continent set between the Pacific and Indian Oceans (map, above), has been extensively settled only along its coastlands. "The Outback" is the name given to the continent's sparsely populated interior —an expanse of plains, deserts and low mountains (shaded areas on map, right). On the Outback's more fertile fringes are savannahs of dwarf eucalypts and acacias (green shading). Farther inland, where rainfall is infrequent and rarely exceeds ten inches a year, the savannahs give way to scrubby grasslands and duned and stony deserts (brown) which embrace the Centre (red)—often called the "Red Centre" because of the predominant colour of its sands. This region, the heart of the Outback, is criss-crossed by the channels of rivers that seldom flow, and dotted by lake beds that hardly ever fill. Here and there the plains of the Centre are studded by monolithic rocky outcrops and ancient mountains, including the Macdonnell Ranges, with their gorges and undulating ridges, and the jagged blue peaks of the Flinders Ranges.

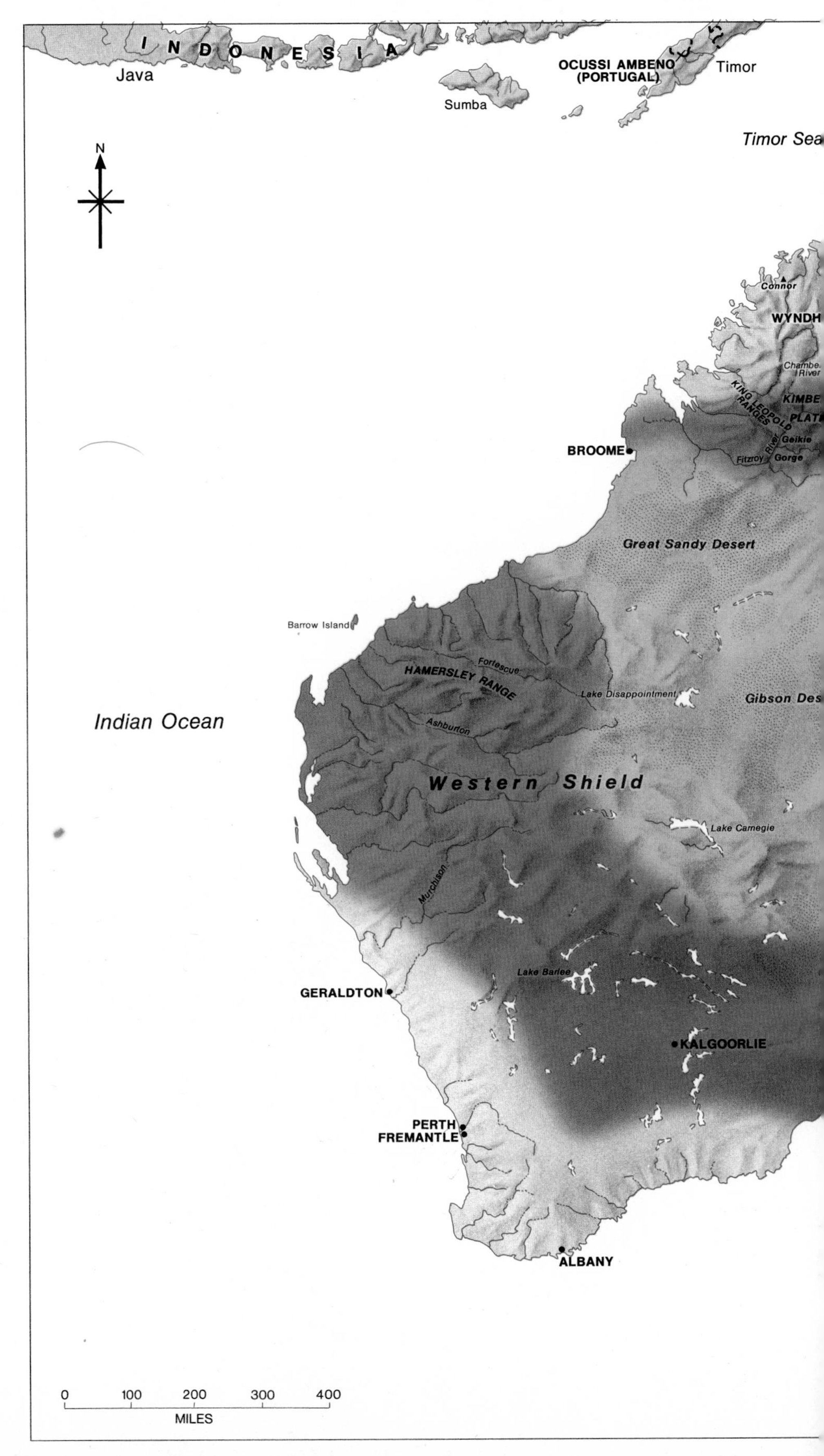

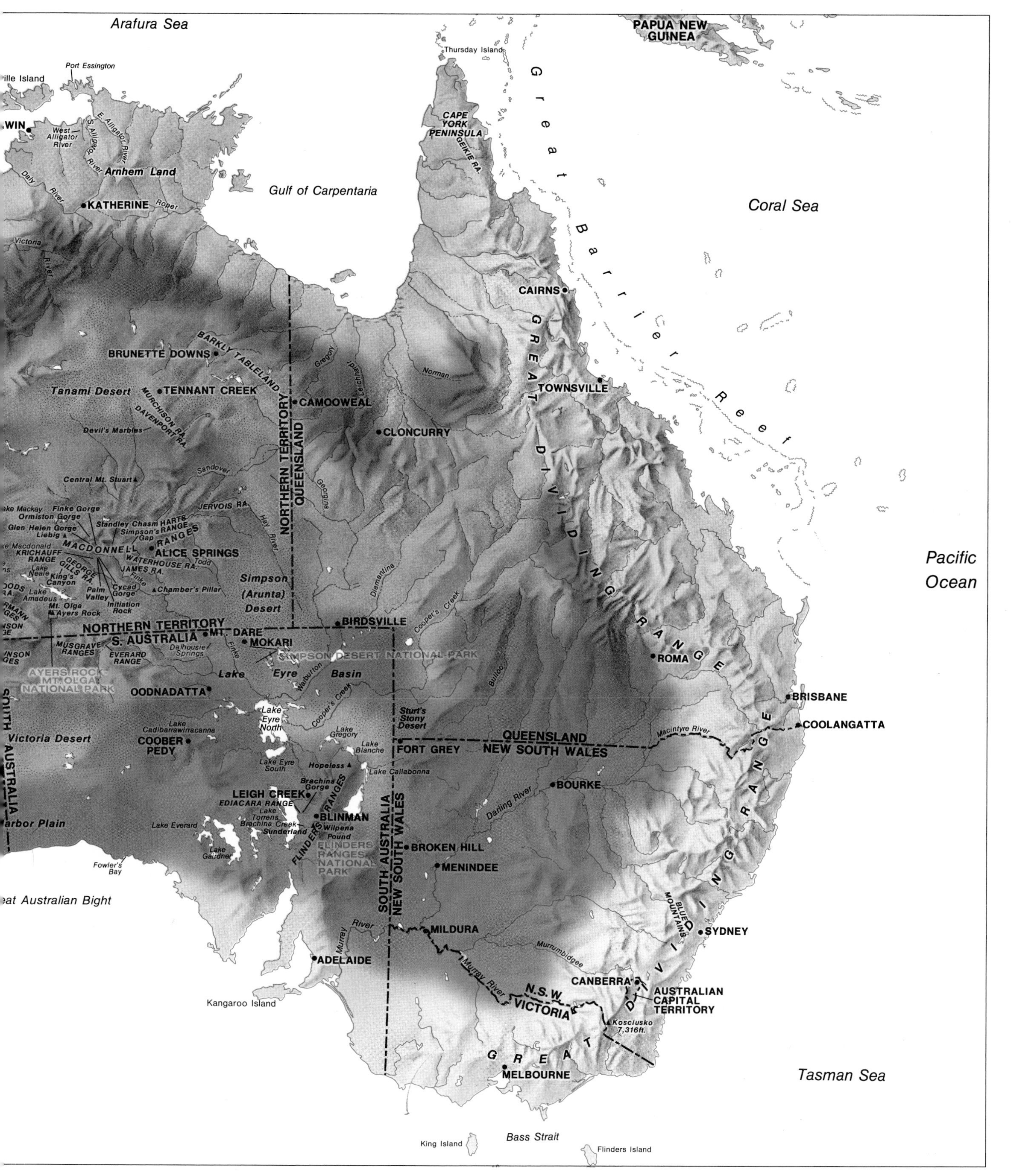
Arafura Sea
Port Essington
Thursday Island
PAPUA NEW GUINEA
CAPE YORK PENINSULA
GEIKIE RA.
Great Barrier Reef
Arnhem Land
West Alligator River
S. Alligator River
E. Alligator River
Daly River
KATHERINE
Roper
Gulf of Carpentaria
Coral Sea
Victoria River
CAIRNS
GREAT DIVIDING RANGE
BARKLY TABLELAND
BRUNETTE DOWNS
Gregory
Leichhardt
Norman
TOWNSVILLE
Tanami Desert
TENNANT CREEK
MURCHISON RA.
DAVENPORT RA.
CAMOOWEAL
CLONCURRY
Devil's Marbles
NORTHERN TERRITORY
QUEENSLAND
Sandover
Georgina
Central Mt. Stuart
JERVOIS RA.
Finke Gorge
Ormiston Gorge
Glen Helen Gorge
Liebig
Standley Chasm
HARTS RANGE
Simpson's Gap
MACDONNELL RANGES
Hay River
KRICHAUFF RANGE
ALICE SPRINGS
WATERHOUSE RA.
Todd
JAMES RA.
Lake Neale
King's Canyon
GEORGE GILL RA
Finke
Simpson (Arunta) Desert
Diamantina
Pacific Ocean
Lake Amadeus
Palm Valley
Cycad Gorge
Chamber's Pillar
Mt. Olga
Ayers Rock
Initiation Rock
Cooper's Creek
BIRDSVILLE
NORTHERN TERRITORY
S. AUSTRALIA
MT. DARE
MOKARI
MUSGRAVE RANGES
EVERARD RANGE
Dalhousie Springs
SIMPSON DESERT NATIONAL PARK
ROMA
AYERS ROCK-MT. OLGA NATIONAL PARK
Lake Eyre Basin
Warburton
Bulloo
OODNADATTA
BRISBANE
Lake Eyre North
Cooper's Creek
Sturt's Stony Desert
Lake Cadibarrawirracanna
Victoria Desert
Lake Gregory
Macintyre River
COOLANGATTA
COOBER PEDY
Lake Blanche
FORT GREY
QUEENSLAND
NEW SOUTH WALES
SOUTH AUSTRALIA
Lake Eyre South
Hopeless
Lake Callabonna
Brachina Gorge
Darling River
BOURKE
LEIGH CREEK
EDIACARA RANGE
Lake Torrens
Brachina Creek
Sunderland
BLINMAN
Wilpena Pound
FLINDERS RANGES
arbor Plain
Lake Everard
Lake Gairdner
FLINDERS RANGES NATIONAL PARK
BROKEN HILL
MENINDEE
SOUTH AUSTRALIA
NEW SOUTH WALES
Fowler's Bay
eat Australian Bight
BLUE MOUNTAINS
SYDNEY
River
Murray
MILDURA
Murrumbidgee
ADELAIDE
Murray River
CANBERRA
AUSTRALIAN CAPITAL TERRITORY
N.S.W.
VICTORIA
Kosciusko 7,316ft.
Kangaroo Island
GREAT DIVIDING RANGE
MELBOURNE
Tasman Sea
King Island
Bass Strait
Flinders Island

1/ Beyond the Black Stump

They call her a young country, but they lie:
She is the last of lands, the emptiest. . . .

A. D. HOPE/ *AUSTRALIA*

The little orange and cream coloured aeroplane climbed up from Sydney and swung away from the east coast of the Australian island continent: away from the foaming lemonade surf exploding on long, golden beaches, the drill squads of volunteer life-savers wheeling and stamping in the sand like so many soldier crabs. It was December, the summer month when Australians flock to the edges of their land, brown bodies massed in mute worship of the sun. We were heading away from them all on a thousand-mile journey inland—the aircraft already bumping and jerking so much in the columns of heat that the very air seemed palpable. We were thrusting back through time to the ancient heart of the continent. Our pilot, a young woman, pointed down at the forested flanks of the Blue Mountains, which rise from the coastal plain about 40 miles west of Sydney. "Take a good look," she said. "That's the last of the hills for a long time."

The Blue Mountains—so-called because of the enveloping haze caused by droplets of eucalyptus oil shining in the atmosphere—are part of the Dividing Range which runs the 2,000-mile length of Australia's east coast. The maze of 4,000-foot peaks and blind gorges we flew over had blocked exploration inland for 25 years after the British settled the continent in 1788. In the early 19th Century, convicts fled from the lash of their Redcoat overseers into these highlands, believing, poor devils, that the Middle Kingdom of China lay beyond the thickly wooded ridges. Few returned: most died of starvation amid the eucalypts or were killed by Aborigines. It was not until 1813 that the first organized explorers found a way across the mountains and saw what lay beyond. Now, in minutes, we crossed this once-formidable barrier, flying low over the deep gorges where high, silvery waterfalls spilled into shady pools, some of which harbour one of Australia's oddest mammals: the egg-laying, milk-producing duck-billed platypus.

Below us the slopes levelled out to merge with the inland plain. In the early 19th Century the plain had been forested, the stands of trees interrupted at intervals by open meadows covered with tall grass. Now the land was neatly broken up into paddocks; flocks of sheep, looking from this height like grains of rice, were scattered over the pastures, and the green pile of the grassy carpet showed yellow geometric patches where wheat flourished. Occasionally we flew over little townships whose corrugated iron roofs glinted like flecks of mica in the sunlight. This is the heartland of the Australian bush tradition; a place where people still tell stories of the pioneer homesteaders who creaked and swayed on bullock carts through the Blue Mountains as they followed in the wake of the 19th-Century explorers. We were going farther than those early settlers did—out into the Centre's Simpson Desert, where no men, not even the Aborigines, live.

For an Australian like myself, a fringe-dweller in a large and empty land, going inland is a little like journeying to the centre of your own being, like tapping the primitive core of your brain. With a colonial history that goes back less than 200 years, and with the scars of a harsh past barely healed, the Australians' true inheritance is the land itself. The reward for birth in the world's most remote inhabited continent is space—nearly 2,000,000 square miles of plains, deserts, scrub, salt lakes and worn-down mountain ranges that make up the Outback. With my wife, Betty, and our 15-year-old son, Dominic, I intended to explore part of this legacy. Our pilot was Alison Edgecombe, a 27-year-old horticulturalist at Sydney's Macquarie University.

We sat riveted by the scene unfolding below. The counterpane pattern of paddocks slowly gave way to a seemingly endless expanse of grey-green shrubs—eucalypts called mallee—and the colours of the earth changed from khaki and green to the inflamed red of sunburnt skin. The landscape was unremittingly flat and steadily grew more arid as we flew on towards the mining town of Broken Hill, 600 miles west of Sydney, where we planned to refuel. In places, the earth was fissured by dry riverbeds, as if gigantic trees had left the imprint of their branches

A strip of scattered mallee trees cuts across the red, spinifex-covered Outback plain north of Broken Hill. The irregular patches of bare sand are the dried beds of shallow pools that fill quickly during the infrequent rainstorms and evaporate within hours under the hot Outback sun.

on it before it was baked hard by the sun. This is the kind of no-man's land where you are wise to drain and clean your radiator, then fill it with fresh water before beginning a journey: you might have to drink the water if you break down. Men stranded in the Outback have wandered away from their vehicles and died of thirst, forgetting that store of water hidden under the bonnet.

The vegetation became even sparser as we flew west. The stands of mallee were succeeded by clumps of mulga, a drought-resistant acacia that is one of the commonest of Outback trees. There seemed to be no haven for humans in that landscape: no wonder so many explorers failed ignominiously to reach the centre of Australia in the last century. Some sought an inland sea in the Outback, a freshwater lake into which the rivers flowing west from the Dividing Range were believed to empty, but their dreams of finding water and grazing land soon evaporated as they trekked across stony plains and parched creek beds. Captain Charles Sturt, the first explorer to search for the fabled body of water, was convinced that the interior "had formerly been an archipelago of islands, and that the apparently boundless plains . . . were the seabeds of the channels".

Sturt's guess was a good one. The interior had been inundated by a succession of seas, but the ancient seabed over which he travelled had been laid bare more than 60 million years ago. Now, even the rivers of the Outback flow only after the rare wet spells and soon trickle away into salt-encrusted marshes or peter out among desert sand dunes. The longest river, the 1,750-mile Darling, came into view beneath one wing; it was no more than a chain of fast-drying lakes stained by the salty dyes of the earth.

Beyond the river there were no towns, only a few isolated homesteads. These homesteaders live "beyond the Black Stump", a mythical place celebrated in Australian folklore as the gateway to the Outback. Their way of life conveys an idea of the immensity of the Outback. The homesteaders' children are not taught locally; they "attend" the School of the Air based at Broken Hill, where teachers using two-way radios broadcast lessons to pupils scattered over half a million square miles of Queensland, New South Wales and South Australia—the most distant child lives more than 450 miles from his "classroom". Each day before school begins, a Strauss waltz gaily wafts in swirls of sound over the plain, then the ragged voices of the children crackle into the ether, bidding their teachers "good morning". Sometimes they join in prayer: "The Lord is my Shepherd; I shall not want. He maketh me to lie down in green pastures: he leadeth me beside still waters." It prickles the skin on my face whenever I hear them recite that psalm, for the green pastures of central Australia withered aeons before Christ.

What impressed me most about the landscape below was its flatness, emptiness, dryness. It was the skeleton of a much older landscape. Australia is one of the most ancient parts of the earth. It is a great slab of land formed early in geological history—more than 3,000 million years ago—and most of its once-high peaks have been worn down to nubs. Only in the Dividing Range are there snow-capped mountains. There, Mount Koskiusco, the highest peak in Australia, reaches 7,316 feet—not an impressive height in a landmass nearly as large as the United States. The plain over which we were flying reaches barely 500 feet above sea-level, about half the average elevation of this, the world's flattest continent.

Outside Antarctica, Australia is also the driest continent, with an overall annual rainfall of little more than 16 inches. Most of the total falls east of the Dividing Range, deluging parts of tropical Queensland with as much as 140 inches a year. Inland it is another story. The crests of the Dividing Range block the moist, warm winds that blow off the Pacific, so that little rain reaches the Outback from the east. In addition, most of inland Australia is right in the "horse latitudes", a zone of dry air recirculated from the tropics. In the Outback itself, which averages less than ten inches a year, occasional clouds that drift down from the monsoon region in the north are the main source of rain.

The ancient heart of this arid zone is the Centre, the focus of my Outback travels. Part of a plateau made up of weathered sedimentary rocks, it covers the southern third of the Northern Territory and the north-east corner of South Australia—some 200,000 square miles in all. On three sides the plains of the Centre merge with immense deserts. In the east is the Simpson Desert, a completely uninhabited expanse of straight, parallel sand dunes of a vivid red—the Centre's dominant colour. Running in an arc along the southern edge of the Centre is the Great Victoria Desert, which turns northwards at the western corner of the Centre to blend with the Gibson Desert. Few roads cut across the Centre, and although it makes up about 10 per cent of the continent, it contains less than 1 per cent of its inhabitants. Here population is measured in square miles per person, not people per square mile.

Most of the Centre is flat and comparatively featureless. Only in the north and south are there mountains worthy of the name. In the north, forming a 200-mile arc east and west of Alice Springs, lie the Macdonnell Ranges: 4,000-foot ridges eroded into undulating folds and dissected—as I would soon see—by deep gorges where a few waterholes support a surprising variety of wildlife. Running into the Centre from the south are the Flinders Ranges: jagged, 3,000-foot peaks where I intended searching for some of the earliest-known fossils.

The Flinders end just south of the Lake Eyre Basin, a low-lying area studded by the glittering salt crusts of dry lake beds. About 500 miles north-west of Lake Eyre the desert plain is punctuated by two mammoth outcrops: Ayers Rock and the Olgas. In 1873 William Gosse, the explorer who discovered Ayers Rock, described in his journal his amazement at seeing the monolithic mass. "When I was only two miles distant, and the hill for the first time coming into view, what was my astonishment to find it was an immense pebble rising abruptly from the plain. This rock is certainly the most wonderful natural feature I have seen." The "pebble" and the near-by summits of the Olgas are now as much a symbol of the Outback for Australians inhabiting the coastal regions as they have been since time immemorial for the Aborigines, who read the story of the Creation in the Rock's strange topography.

The plants and animals that manage to live in the Centre have adapted to desert conditions, and their variety is an affirmation of life. Seeds lie buried in the parched sand between brief periods of flowering; frogs bury themselves in the ground with an internal supply of water to

A fat-tailed dunnart, one of the many small marsupials of the Outback, chews on a gecko it has just caught. Although it is not much bigger than a domestic mouse, the dunnart is a fierce, nocturnal carnivore that preys on small birds, mice and centipedes. It stores excess food in its tail as fat, drawing upon this reserve during lean times.

tide them over droughts (the Aborigines dig them out and squeeze them to slake a thirst); some small marsupials store food reserves in their large tails, and others go into a dormant state during the summer months. To escape the fierce heat of the sun most creatures of the Centre are nocturnal; often the only signs of their presence—as I would discover to my frustration—are the scattered tracks that mark the sand. During the day the desert plain looks empty, lifeless under the burning sun, and the only shadows in the sky are birds of prey silently riding the thermals on splay-tipped wings.

Before the Centre dried up, it was a fertile region. One hundred and fifty million years ago, during the Jurassic Period, it was covered with jungle and dotted with freshwater lakes in which dinosaurs wallowed. At that time Australia was located far to the south of its present position and was fused with India, Africa, South America and Antarctica to form the supercontinent of Gondwanaland. When Gondwanaland began to split up and drift apart, about a hundred million years ago, South America and Africa were the first to break off (the shape of their present Atlantic coastlines suggests how they were once joined, like the interlocking pieces of a jigsaw puzzle). At about the same time, the landmass that would become Australia was inundated by a shallow sea that divided it from north to south. Marine reptiles swam where now salt pans shimmer. One of them, a plesiosaur named *Kronosaurus*, was 42 feet long, with a nine-foot head armed with ranks of teeth. *Kronosaurus* was the largest flesh-eating marine reptile known, but it was one of the last of its kind—a grand finale of the era of giant reptiles.

Australia broke away from what remained of Gondwanaland about 45 million years ago and moved slowly northwards. The newly isolated island continent was like a gigantic Ark, carrying on board a menagerie of primitive mammals as well as an assembly of other animals and plants. Most of the mammals were marsupials: creatures born in a foetal state that complete their early development in their mother's external pouch, which is equipped with teats for suckling. The more advanced placental mammals, which evolved mainly in the northern continents, did not reach Australia until much later. Thus the continent's marsupials were able to evolve and diversify in ecological niches from which in other lands they were soon ousted.

As Australia drifted slowly northwards, its climate changed. About six to 11 million years ago a large ice cap formed in the Antarctic. Sea level fell as water was taken up from the oceans and added to the ice cap, and the temperature of the Southern Ocean around Australia dropped. Then came the great Ice Ages of the Pleistocene. As the atmosphere cooled, the winds became stronger over Australia, increasing evaporation. Inland lakes dried up, the vegetation of Central Australia withered, and sand dunes, shaped by the strong winds, were formed. Out of such dynamic change had come the landscape over which Alison was now piloting us.

During that period, Australia drifted close to its present position, near the south-east tip of Asia. Placental mammals gained a foothold on the continent, reaching it by island "stepping stones" or via a land-bridge that perhaps temporarily connected the two landmasses. Bats and rodents streamed into Australia. Finally, Aboriginal man arrived from Asia, less than 40,000 years ago. Later waves of immigrants brought with them a semi-domesticated dog, the dingo, which running wild became Australia's largest land predator of today.

One of the immigrants from Asia was a tiny freshwater fish, the desert hardyhead. It was discovered as recently as 1967 in a hot-spring oasis called Dalhousie Springs, on the south-west corner of the Simpson Desert, about 75 miles north of the township of Oodnadatta. Hardyheads are not much to look at—tiddlers two and a half inches long, of the sort fishermen use as bait. However, their significance is far greater than their size. They are found nowhere else in Australia; their closest relatives live in New Guinea. How they got to the Centre no one knows for certain; they may have been transported as eggs clinging to the legs of birds. When the rivers of the Centre dried up they were stranded at Dalhousie. For me, the desert hardyheads symbolize the tenacity of life in the Outback; and so, when I planned my journey I decided that my first goal would be the hot pools at Dalhousie Springs.

After refuelling at Broken Hill, Alison piloted our aeroplane north-west over terrain that became grimmer with every passing mile. The grey-green carpet of mulga scrub frayed to an end and was succeeded by corrugated, pink sand ridges daubed with clumps of spinifex grass. Red "willy-willys"—spiralling columns of dust whipped up by the wind—danced across the desert. Soon we were crossing one of the driest parts of Australia, the Lake Eyre Basin, which receives a scant five inches of rain a year. Far away on the eastern horizon, we could see a strip of land that looked like an abstract canvas smeared black and green, and streaked white where salt beds glittered. This was Lake Callabonna, the salt-pan graveyards of hundreds of *Diprotodons*: two-ton, plant-eating marsupials that perished more than 25,000 years ago.

'ater-cut gullies vein a low-lying dune in New South Wales. The dune is made up of wind-blown deposits from the dried-up bed of near-by Lake Mungo.

Here, during the Pleistocene, when the changing climate of Australia spelt their extinction, some of the last specimens of *Diprotodons* floundered in their death throes after struggling vainly to reach an artesian spring in the drying clay bed of Lake Callabonna. Hundreds lay buried under a crust of lime and gypsum until in 1892 an Aborigine reported their remains to a pioneer sheep farmer, Fred Ragless. Ragless rode his horse out on to the lake bed and was amazed to see giant skeletons scattered over several acres, with skulls nearly three feet long and rib-ends sticking out of the mud.

The South Australian Museum sent an expedition to the graveyard the following year, and one of the party even found a *Diprotodon* that had died with its young. "As soon as I had dug under the pelvis," he wrote excitedly, "and into the exact spot where the pouch would be, I came on a dear little *Diprotodon* humerus about six inches long. . . . The claim is very wet and the bones are difficult to remove, but you can depend I will get them all as I think this is the most wonderful discovery ever made in the world." The expedition counted 360 skeletons on the surface and managed to remove more than 70 of them before hunger and thirst forced them to abandon their collecting.

Other expeditions have visited the lake since, including a joint American-Australian group in 1970, which began work at the 1893 site and within half an hour had found three *Diprotodon* skeletons simply by prodding with steel probes. The expedition also discovered skeletons of giant kangaroos and wombats, and evidence of a lakeside forest that had flourished before the rainfall dwindled. "The scientific potential of Lake Callabonna still remains largely unexplored," reported a member of the group. "There is not another site like it in the world."

Lake Callabonna slipped out of sight, and I peered through the heat-haze for a first glimpse of Lake Eyre, where the ambitions of many Outback explorers faltered as they tried to cross its crust of powdery, gypseous silt. "All who have travelled there have felt this haunting sense of desolation and death," wrote Dr. C. T. Madigan, a geologist and explorer who visited the area in 1939. "The song dies on the drover's lips; silence falls on the exploring party. It is like entering a vast tomb; one hesitates to break the silence. The rivers are dead, the trees are dead, but overshadowing all in the qualities of death is the very heart of the region, the great lake itself, a horrible travesty, a vast, white, prostrate giant of a lake. Here time seems to have stood still for ages, and all is dead. . . . The Dead Heart, the focus of a drainage basin of 450,000 square miles of country will never throb again."

An Australian pelican preens itself by the shore of an inland lake in south-west Queensland. The species keeps its plumage clean and waterproof by using its bill to spread a thin layer of oil over its feathers. The oil is secreted by a gland at the base of the pelican's tail.

But Madigan's pessimistic prediction was not borne out. After an unusually wet summer in 1949-1950, rivers that had been dry for years coursed into the main body of Lake Eyre, provoking dreams of a lush new age in the interior. It was a false promise: the sun, evaporating moisture at the rate of a hundred inches a year, soon sucked the lake dry, allowing Donald Campbell to set a new world land speed record on the salt flats there in his car, Bluebird, in 1964. Geologists, who rode out on to the lake bed on balloon-tyred motor tricycles, thought the lake would not fill again in their lifetime, but they were wrong. In 1974, after phenomenally heavy rains, the water was up to 20 feet deep where Campbell had raced and, for the first time in living memory, it poured through a narrow channel into Lake Eyre South.

With the water came wildlife. Flocks of wood ducks, grey teal and white-backed swallows returned to breed. Cockatoos, such as corellas and galahs, screeched along the banks, and pelicans glided importantly over the lake surface as if they had been there forever. A four-man expedition in two punts set out to cross the lake and, although one of the punts capsized, the men did make a little bit of history: the first recorded boat crossing—in 1974!—of Australia's largest lake.

Suddenly, there it was below us: a jade-green inland sea swollen by the recent heavy rains—a sea seemingly brimming with enough water to last for years. It was not fresh, as in ancient times, but it was, in its way, a miracle. The "Dead Heart" that Dr. Madigan had described had revived. As our aeroplane raced above the lake, the roar of its engines disturbed thousands of silver gulls that had established breeding colonies on the shore. It was an astonishing sight—seagulls nesting in a desert, 400 miles from the sea.

The aeroplane passed over the lake and began to buck over the baking salt flats that lie between the water's edge and the sand dunes of the Simpson Desert. The landscape changed abruptly: one minute the earth was beige and cracked by the sun like crazy paving, the next it was ribbed by roseate sand ridges and veined by the clotted artery of an occasional sluggish river. We flew a hundred miles north-west along the edge of the Simpson before we saw Oodnadatta below us, a shabby little outpost that we planned to use as a base while we searched for the desert hardyhead. Kites flapped away from the airstrip as we landed. We climbed stiffly out of the aeroplane to be met by a blast of hot air. Tying down the aircraft to protect it from wind squalls, we were exposed for the first time to the Outback sun—a taste of the purgatory to come.

My first dismal impression of Oodnadatta was reinforced when I learned that the township was infested by a plague of long-haired rats, which sporadically "erupt" out of the bush in years of plenty, rather like arctic lemmings. Aborigines, the remnants of broken tribes, wandered down the dusty main street, their plangent dialects sounding like the clatter of strange birds. Fortunately, the local postmaster, storekeeper and bush pilot, Jaroslav Pecanek, turned out to be a friendly man who, when we told him we were going to Dalhousie Springs next day, promised to fly out and find us if we did not return safely.

"Peck", as he was known, a former accountant from Czechoslovakia, had a fund of Outback tales. He told us, for example, that he had suffered so badly from sinusitis when living in Adelaide that his doctor had advised him to emigrate to the Sahara. Instead, he said with a straight face, he had chosen Oodnadatta. Peck had made more than a thousand landings in the Centre and nonchalantly described some of the hazards of Outback flying—like navigating through the suction created by a bushfire, "climbing on full power and going down a thousand feet a minute". He also told us of his efforts to photograph a herd of wild camels in the Simpson, buzzing so low over one angry old bull that he could see the beast's eyes rolling as it reared up at the aeroplane. "When I landed," he said, "there was spit on the wing."

We did not sleep well that night. The bush rats ran over our beds and it was a relief to get up next morning. The rising sun was a bright orange ball sliced neatly in two by a distant plume of bushfire smoke as Alison and I took off for Dalhousie Springs. Betty and Dominic stayed behind; there was no sense in them taking the risk, no matter how slight, of visiting a place so wild that it is officially designated a "Remote Area"—and the aircraft would be lighter for desert take-offs. We headed along the western edge of the Simpson, and touched down about a hundred miles north of Oodnadatta at a lonely cattle station called Mount Dare. We wanted to ask the owner, Rex Lowe, for permission to land at the hot springs, which were on his extensive property. The homestead looked deserted as we walked from the airstrip and it was some time before Mr. Lowe answered our knocks. He told us that he had been sending an emergency call to the Outback's Flying Doctor: "I've got a sick black boy," he told us. "Keep's hearing voices and answering." Mr. Lowe was a quintessential Outback bushman: tough and stringy, with pale blue eyes narrowed against the glare of the sun. Yes, he said, we were welcome to visit Dalhousie Springs, which was about 30 miles from his homestead.

He told us that the recent rains had been the heaviest he had known in 36 years in the Centre. Knowing that, during our final hop over a landscape of red sand and white, baked clay pans, I could hardly imagine what it must be like during a drought. Mount Dare cattle station exists only because it lies on the western rim of the world's largest artesian basin, a 500,000-square-mile subterranean lake that occupies most of the south-east corner of Australia. The basin is a vast drainage sink fed by the rivers that flow from the Dividing Range and the mountains of the Centre. Where the water is confined under presure, it escapes in rare places to form "mound springs": miniature volcano-like structures that build up as minerals are precipitated from the hot water. These mound springs feed the hot pools where the desert hardyheads live.

Passing low over the crumbling yellow walls and ancient date palms of an abandoned homestead, we landed bumpily beside the main pool at Dalhousie Springs. The thermometer in the cabin registered nearly 130° F., and the buckle of my seat-belt burnt my legs as I unclipped it. Alison and I dropped down on to the sand and stood for a moment or two under the shade of one wing to get used to the heat, then we walked across to the pool, a ribbon of water about 30 yards wide. I squelched across the gluey, black mud until I could swim out to the middle of the pool, treading water, but it was about as refreshing as a warm bath. I waded back, climbed out and pushed through thick clumps of tea trees, the honey-sweet scent of their yellow flowers mingling with the chemical tang of the mineral-rich pool.

A black duck, startled by my intrusion, plunged into the water and hidden animals rustled through the scrub. I made plenty of noise to frighten off snakes, although I was aware that the death adder, one of the most lethal of Australia's 70 venomous species, rarely moves aside from danger. At last I broke through the scrub to a tiny stream of clear, hot water that issued from a mound spring hidden in a thicket. Following the stream, I found that it ran into the pool I had just left. At its outlet blue dragonflies darted above the water, on which a few hawk feathers floated amid wisps of algae. I sat down by a strange bone as large as a propeller—a camel's, perhaps—and peered into the water.

The fish that I had come so far to see belongs to the genus *Craterocephalus*, and is unique in being the only member of the genus that is sexually dimorphic—which means that you can distinguish male and female just by looking at them. The female has a concave forehead and a flat belly, while the male is more streamlined and bulbous underneath. But more than that, they are able to survive in temperatures that would kill most other fish. They spend most of their lives in the spring-fed pools, which range in temperature from a modest 74° F. to a perilously warm 104° F. In the pool I was watching, however, they brave temperatures of up to 100° F. when they dash into the hot feeder stream to grab mouthfuls of blue-green algae that grow there. In this unlikely habitat the desert hardyheads cling to survival: the few scattered pools at Dalhousie, mere specks in the desert, are their entire world.

I watched the junction of the stream for an hour, but no fish appeared. The sun mounted higher, the day grew hotter. I was on the point of abandoning my watch when there was a flash of silver at the head of the pool. Something small and gleaming darted from the depths, hesitated at the mouth of the stream, then dashed into the hot, bubbling current. I waited for the performance to be repeated, but nothing stirred; and eventually the heat forced me to return to the aeroplane. Had I seen a desert hardyhead, or had my eyes been deceived by some trick of the dazzling light? I could not be sure but, somehow, I felt no disappointment. No traveller should barge into the Australian Outback expecting to stumble on its wonders. The first lesson is patience: I would remember this on the next part of my journey, when I ventured into the sand dunes of the Simpson.

I stumbled back to the aircraft and swigged hot water from a flask in the cabin. Two miles away, across white salt pans, another pool lay amid a clump of date palms that had sprouted, perhaps, from seeds tossed aside by Afghan camel drivers in the exploring days. I thought about searching that pool for the elusive fish. But although I knew I could have walked there, I doubted my ability to get back. "You wouldn't make it in this heat," Alison warned me, and so we decided to return to Oodnadatta. Back in the township I felt so groggy from exposure to the sun that I had to sit on the wheel of the aeroplane for 20 minutes, my head pounding. I could not think clearly; I just stared stupidly at the red earth, an image of a hot, blue pool filled with secret fish burning in my brain.

The Centre's Worn Face

The central Australian landscape is one of the earth's most ancient and, seen from the air, it displays its age as clearly as the haggard face of an old man. The mountains of what Australians call the Centre were middle-aged by the time of the dinosaurs, and now they are weathered stumps that wrinkle the dry skin of the desert plain. The Centre's rivers flowed before life emerged on land; now they are hardened arteries choked by sand for most of the year.

A traveller flying across the Centre is impressed first of all by its flatness: a sure sign of age. After great convulsions, mountains rose to great heights more than 400 million years ago; then the Centre settled back into a repose that was barely disturbed by later, gentle movements of the earth's crust. Over the aeons the eroding forces of wind, water and ice gnawed irresistibly at the mountains, levelling slopes, smoothing contours and grinding down mighty peaks to the stubby ridges that crease the Centre today.

Seen on the ground, the Centre appears largely featureless, with little vegetation to clothe its rocky frame. Its empty expanses inspire awe and sometimes fear, for there are few landmarks to guide the traveller. Viewed from the air, however, the land presents a strange geometry of patterns, thrown into bold relief by the harsh light. Desert sand ridges resemble the waves of a petrified sea, rock outcrops run straight as Roman roads and, separated by great plains, ridges of the few remaining mountain ranges rise and fall with the regularity of tombstones in a cemetery.

Red is the predominant colour of the Centre, for each particle of soil is coated with a layer of "rust"—iron oxides that are by-products of weathering in arid regions. Only when enough rain falls to stimulate plant growth does the Centre lose its rusty finish. Then, seeds that have lain dormant germinate and sprout, cloaking the land with a short-lived flourish of green. At the same time, dried up rivers flow again.

But these bursts of life are sporadic. The sun soon bakes the plains dry; the rivers diminish to a trickle that vanishes into the sand. Without the force of run-off water to shape the landscape, the Centre relapses into immobility. Perhaps another mountain-building era will one day galvanize it into fresh activity. In the meantime it is wrapped in a geological calm.

Like ridges turned up by a giant plough, red longitudinal dunes stripe the Simpson Desert south-east of Alice Springs. The dunes, which are as much as a hundred feet high, are aligned parallel with the prevailing south-easterly wind. Each uncompacted crest rests on a core of consolidated sand.

An unaccustomed covering of greenery (above) cloaks looping sandhills near Ayers Rock, in an area where there is no constant prevailing wind to impose a regular dune pattern. Unusually heavy rains have triggered off the growth of dormant desert plants.

Winding gullies (left) have been etched between the ridges of the Simpson Desert by corkscrewing air currents flowing in the direction of the camera. Each Y-junction was formed when a vortex rose from the ground, and a neighbouring eddy cut across to join its path.

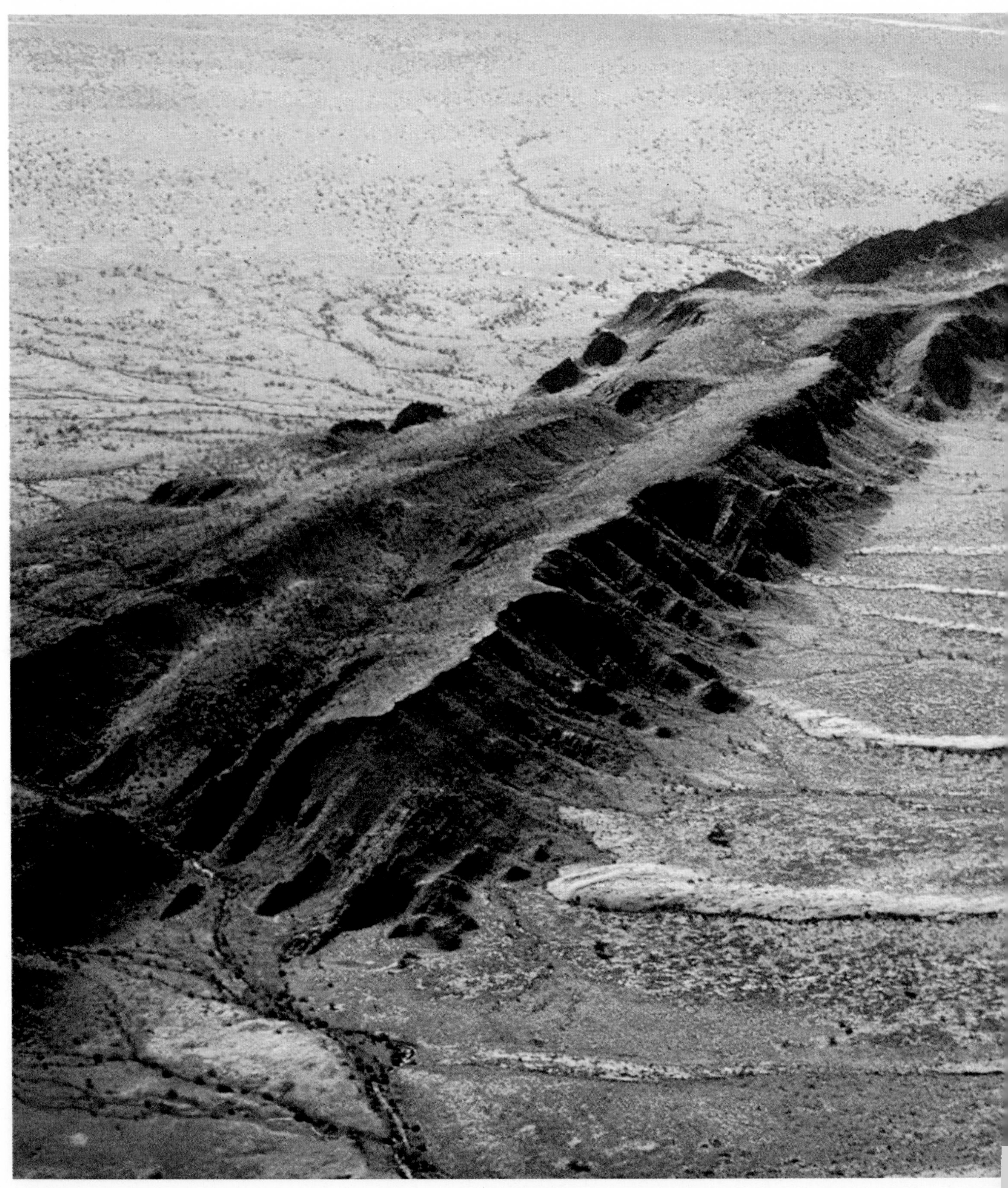

An ancient quartzite outcrop of the Macdonnell Ranges cuts through longitudinal dunes on the Simpson Desert's northern edge. On each side of the outcrop, clumps of spinifex turned green by rains pin-cushion the sand. The meandering lines of darker green vegetation reveal where water remains under the beds of now-dry streams.

Like giant wheel ruts, a pair of parallel valleys (right) run between corrugated ridges of the Macdonnell Ranges. The valleys were formed when running water scoured away beds of soft shale and sandstone, isolating the resistant quartzite ridges—all that is left of a once mighty chain of mountains.

The curious undulations of a ridge in the Macdonnells (above) bear witness to a complex pattern of erosion. Streams running at right angles to the main valleys have cut across the grain of the clearly defined rock beds, carving the ridge into a series of rounded humps that are known locally as tombstones.

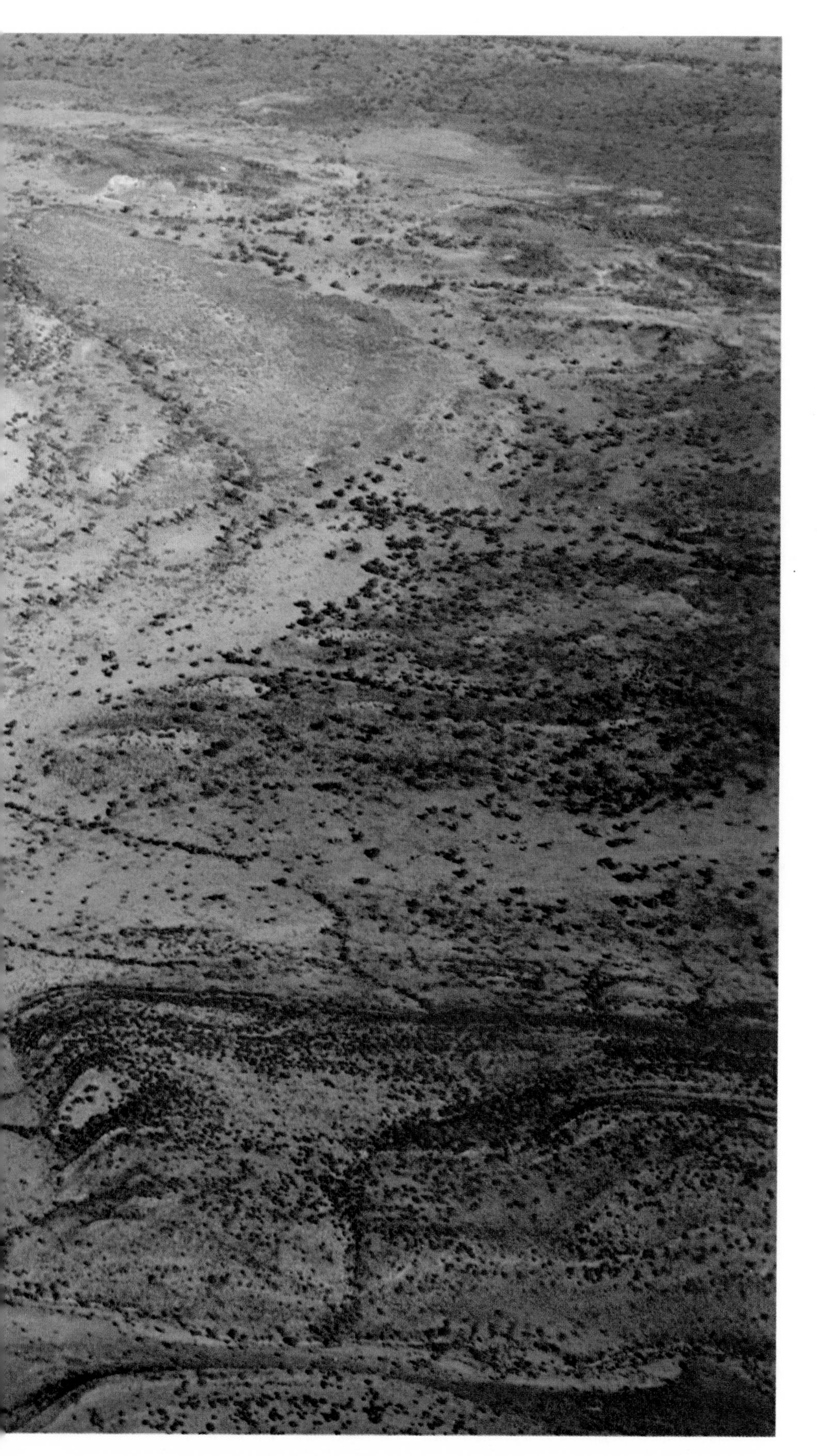

The sluggish waters of the Finke river, central Australia's longest watercourse, cut a sandy channel through scrubland south of the Macdonnell Ranges. Although the river is usually dry, a layer of moisture always remains beneath its channels, providing sustenance for the deep-rooted shrubs on its banks and justifying the name the Aborigines give it: Larapinta, or "permanent water".

Sandy, salt-rimmed islands dot the dry bed of Lake Amadeus, south of the Macdonnells. Occasionally the lake fills and as its waters evaporate,

salts are precipitated in rings around the islands. The paler, least soluble salts are deposited first; the darker, more soluble salts last.

2/ The Fiery Gridiron

Well into the 20th Century, one vast area of Australia still defied the explorer. This was the desert later called the Simpson . . . " WILLIAM JOY/ *THE EXPLORERS*

After returning to Oodnadatta from Dalhousie Springs, the tiny oasis on the western fringe of the Simpson Desert, I resolved to experience, if only briefly, the desert's unsheltered impact; to wander in that wilderness of sand and silence where the dunes rise like rows of houses in a deserted city. The evening before our flight into the Simpson, I strolled to the northern outskirts of Oodnadatta, where a tribe of Aborigines had an encampment on the stony plain surrounding the town. I found a group of them huddled together, their backs turned to the desert which, in Aboriginal lore, is a land of death peopled by evil spirits. Gazing beyond the group, I, too, felt a fearful respect for the distant, glowering waste which retained its secrets long after the rest of the Outback had been explored and mapped.

With an aeroplane to lift us over the dunes and a radio link to the outside world, we faced little risk from the Simpson. Nevertheless, I could not shake off a feeling of uneasiness. It was strong enough to make me leave my wife Betty and son Dominic behind in Oodnadatta when Alison and I took off early the next morning for the desert airstrip of Mokari, some hundred miles to the north-east.

Within minutes we were winging over the Simpson's rose-pink sand ridges. Unlike the sinuous, constantly shifting dunes of deserts such as the Sahara, most of those in the Simpson are heaped into fixed longitudinal ridges. Running N. 30° W., there are more than a thousand of them, covering a total area of about 56,000 square miles, from Lake Eyre in South Australia to the eastern ramparts of the Macdonnell Ranges in the Northern Territory. Some of these stationary dunes stretch in unbroken succession for as much as 75 miles, rising to heights of up to 150 feet. Rainfall over this area is barely four inches a year and, although streams flow into the Simpson from the north-west after heavy downpours, the water quickly evaporates or disappears into the sand.

Dr. C. T. Madigan, an Australian geologist and explorer who made the first survey flights over the Simpson in 1929, gave a dramatic description of its torrid landscape. "The whole expanse below," he wrote, "was like a pink and gigantic circular gridiron ribbed with close, straight sand ridges from horizon to horizon." Skimming low over the "gridiron", we spotted Mokari airstrip, a mere thumbnail scored between two 50-foot-high dunes which ran straight as tramlines into the heat-haze. Hacked out years before by an oil company and then abandoned when the search for wealth beneath the sands proved fruitless, the strip had been partly recolonized by spinifex and we swished to a bumpy halt through the scattered clumps.

Climbing out of the aeroplane, we felt the silence close about us, as intense and tangible as the scorching heat. The late morning sun was already pushing the mercury towards 100° F. and bothered me more than it did Alison. Foolishly, I had forgotten to bring a hat, but Alison rummaged in the aeroplane and eventually brought me a large straw boater adorned with a gay blue band. I clapped it on gratefully and set off alone towards the nearest dune, moving with the clumsy caution of an astronaut who has just stepped on to the surface of an unknown planet. Although the ridges in this part of the Simpson are no more than 300 yards apart, I found it hard going on the desert floor. The loose sand plucked at my feet, and clumps of spinifex drew blood whenever I stumbled against their needle-sharp leaf-blades.

I found climbing easier than walking. The Simpson ridges rise steeply from the north-east, but from the south-west they slope more gently, and since the latter was the side I had chosen to ascend, I soon reached the first crest. Looking back towards the airstrip I saw the distant figure of Alison bending down beside the aeroplane to collect plant specimens. The view ahead was less reassuring. Row after row of dunes stretched away to the horizon. The only contrast to the red sand was provided by patches of grey-green vegetation along the crests of the ridges and in the valleys between.

I was scanning the near-by vegetation for signs of life when I heard

Ripples pattern a fiery red sand dune, one of more than a thousand parallel ridges that rib the Simpson Desert at quarter-mile intervals.

a sound like tinkling bells. It was the song of some small desert birds—possibly white-winged wrens—that were flitting away through the low scrub. Following their music down the far side of the ridge, I came to a dwarf acacia and was startled to see a brown falcon perched on an upper branch, idly preening itself. The bird seemed quite unconcerned by my presence and waited until I was almost within touching distance before flying away. Unused to humans, it was simply not conditioned to regard them as an immediate threat.

Clambering down the steep face of the dune left me panting, so I rested for a while beside a cluster of white daisies, *Helipterum floribundum*. Like many other desert plants, the daisies bloom profusely after rain and then die off, leaving their seeds to lie dormant in the sand until the next downpour. I plucked at the parched flowers and they crumbled between my fingers likes ashes. It seemed ironic that this landscape was once covered by a sea.

Throughout most of the Mesozoic Period, between 70 million and 180 million years ago, the low-lying area of eastern central Australia, including what is now the Simpson, was inundated. Sea-water invading from the Gulf of Carpentaria in the north ebbed and flowed over the land, and vast lakes were formed by rivers pouring from the highlands to the east and west. Eventually, geological upheavals altered the drainage pattern of the area. The sea ebbed for the last time, the lakes dried up and aridity set in. Fierce winds then tore at the sediments that had been deposited by the water, scattering fine particles of clay towards Australia's southern and eastern coasts and heaping the heavier grains of quartzite into the Simpson's sand dunes.

Now, when rain descends on the desert, the water either evaporates or sinks straight into the sand, where it is absorbed by the roots of hardy plants. But deep beneath the sand lies steadily accumulating rain-water that trickles off the mountains far to the north-east. Trapped between the bedrock and the upper strata of sediment, this water collects many thousands of feet below its intake point and is under intense and constant pressure, so that any break in the top rock layer causes it to gush in steaming jets to the surface. In some places it erupts in natural aqueous volcanoes known as mound springs; in others it spurts from man-made artesian bores. Here in the Simpson, however, the water remains locked beneath the scorched sand, as useless to the sweating traveller as a mirage on the shimmering horizon.

Toiling over the dunes and through the intervening valleys, where the spinifex continually stabbed my legs, was exhausting work—and all the more so in the desert heat. I tried to offset my discomfort by searching the sand for animal tracks. Knowing how to read tracks is a matter of crucial importance to the Aborigines who live on the desert's fringes. They show their children how to identify the tracks, using the sands as a natural schoolroom. A baby's bottom pressed in smooth sand, for example, will supply the outline of a camel track. The children are also taught to follow human tracks. Aboriginal mothers hide among the dunes and force their children to find them by following the clues written in the sand. The other tribefolk do not give the mothers away, merely pointing at the marked ground when the wails become desperate. It is a hard school, but one designed for an even harder world.

Lacking the expertise of the Aborigines, I was unable to identify many of the tracks I did see. But several times I recognized the imprints of dingoes and snakes, and once I came across signs of a camel, a wild descendant of those brought from Africa in the 19th Century to aid explorers of Australia's interior. It was consoling to find evidence of life in the midst of such seeming desolation, and the sense of apprehension that had haunted me since my encounter with the Aborigines of Oodnadatta began to fade. Here in the Simpson, as in all environments, the survivors are those that have learned how to adapt. Heat and drought are the desert's chief hazards and each species has evolved its own method of coping. Many, like the hopping mice and the carnivorous marsupial mice, remain in cool underground burrows during the heat of the day, emerging only at night to hunt for food. The hopping mice are particularly well-adapted to survive since they obtain all the moisture they need from a diet of seeds, and may go through the whole of their lives without drinking any water.

One of the rarest and least studied of the underground dwellers is the tiny marsupial mole. When the first specimen was discovered under a spinifex tussock in 1888, it caused great excitement among naturalists and zoologists, for it supported Darwin's still controversial ideas about convergent evolution. This means that although the placental mole developed from quite different stock, it bears striking resemblances—in form and behaviour—to its namesakes in the Northern Hemisphere and Africa. This indicates that unrelated species develop along convergent lines when faced with similar needs and challenges.

Because the marsupial mole is so difficult to find, little is known of its habits in the wild; two individuals that were studied in captivity, however, displayed the same behaviour as placental moles, continually alternating between feverish activity and torpid slumber, without any transitional phase. They were kept in a box of sand in which they burrowed, but they did not construct permanent tunnels or leave passageways behind them. Instead they "swam" through the sand with a breast-stroke action of the forelimbs.

During their waking hours, the captured specimens fed ravenously on insects and larvae as if trying to cram as much eating into the time as possible. But during sleep their metabolism dropped so low that they could have gone for prolonged periods without any food at all. Many desert creatures—including some species of insects—take this principle of energy-conservation-through-sleep a stage further, spending the hottest and driest months in a state of dormancy, and waking only when the rains have brought forth fresh plant-growth.

In spite of appearances, therefore, life is not absent from the Simpson, but often merely hidden, biding its time, waiting for rain or darkness to come. Even the spiteful spinifex is an affirmation of the tenacity—and interdependence—of this unseen world; for in the centre of the spiked tussocks many species of birds, insects, snakes, lizards and small mammals find refuge from sun, wind and predators. The desert offers no such shelter to humans, however, and there were those for whom the Simpson did, indeed, become a land of death. I reflected on what it would be like to be alone here, and—for a moment, with Alison and the aircraft out of sight—I tensed once more with apprehension.

No one knows for sure how many explorers, stockmen and prospectors have perished in the desert, hopelessly yearning for a pool or a spring beyond the next ridge. But gruesome tales abound. In 1900, for example, three stockmen taking a short cut across a corner of the Simpson slashed the throats of their horses and drank the blood in a final, desperate bid to survive. They died. Another stockman, returning with liquor and groceries from the lonely township of Birdsville on the south-eastern edge of the desert, drank two dozen bottles of whisky after his horse had wandered off and left him stranded. Searchers found him dead surrounded by empties.

Dr. Madigan's aerial survey in 1929 simply confirmed what most people had always suspected: that the Simpson could never be crossed on foot. Standing alone amid the intimidating dunes, I found it easy to understand their point of view. But Edmund A. Colson, a settler living in a remote homestead at Bloods Creek, west of Oodnadatta, refused to accept that the Simpson could never be crossed. "Give me a good season, a blackfellow who'll do what I tell him, and a few good camels," he

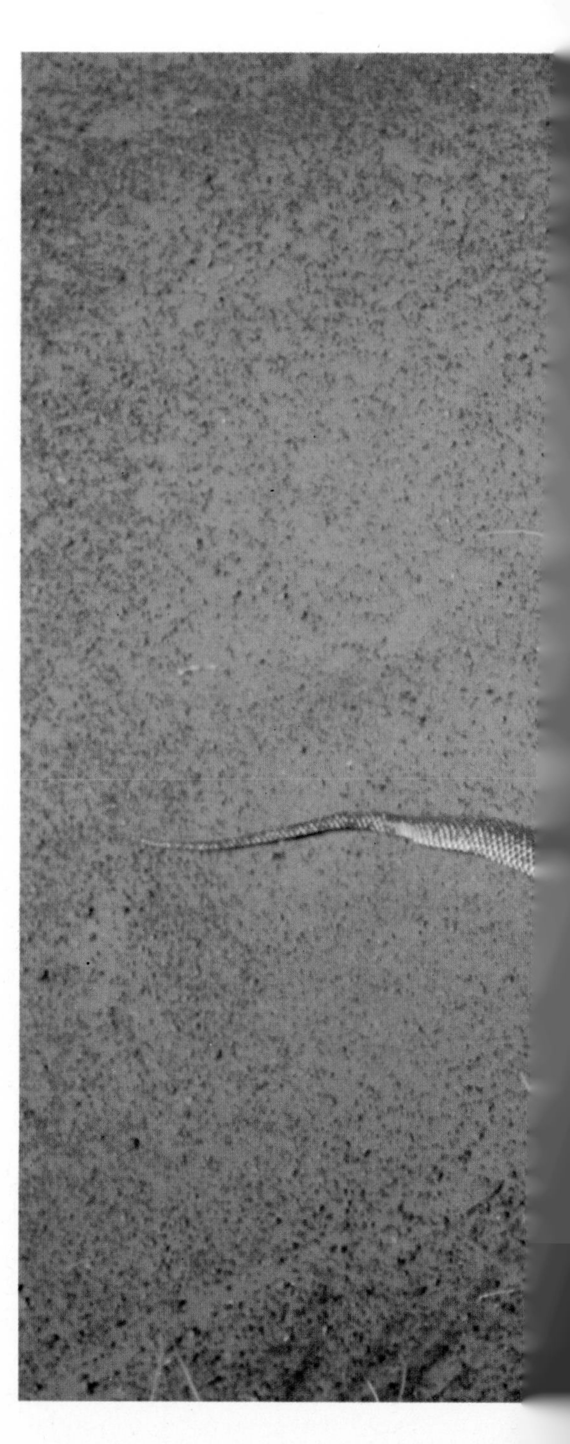

A venomous, six-foot-long mulga snake glides across red Outback soil. The snake's thick neck identifies it as an old specimen.

declared in 1929, "and I'll do it myself." Colson believed that, given sufficient rain, millions of seeds that were lying dormant in the sand would be germinated, thereby providing enough food and moisture to sustain an expedition.

For seven years he waited; and then, at last, an unusually heavy storm broke, and he set off from Bloods Creek with an Aborigine named Peter, five camels and a month's supply of food and water. Colson was aiming for Birdsville, 200 miles to the north-east, across the Simpson's southern extremities. As he pressed on, the dunes got progressively higher, and sometimes the camels were forced to struggle on their knees over the steep, loosely packed crests. By day, the two men sweltered in temperatures of more than 100° F.; at night, they shivered in temperatures below freezing. But on the third day Colson's great gamble paid off. Cresting a ridge, he saw parakeelya spread like a great purple carpet on the floor of the valley below.

The most prolific and spectacular of the desert plants, parakeelya is a fleshy herb of the *Calandrinia* genus and retains water in its jelly-like fronds. Colson's camels gorged themselves on the succulent plants and, according to his own account, they were soon frisking like lambs. The expedition came upon other widely scattered oases of life-giving shrubs, and only 16 days after leaving Bloods Creek, they plodded into Birdsville and halted outside the hotel. At first, the townspeople refused to believe they had crossed the Simpson, remaining unconvinced until the photographs Colson had taken were developed. Colson himself remained cool and unconcerned. After a short rest, he saddled up his camels again and recrossed the desert to Bloods Creek.

In 1939 Dr. Madigan, whose earlier survey flights over the Simpson had inspired Colson's epic conquest, led his own expedition across the centre of the desert. Equipped with 19 camels and a two-way radio, Madigan and seven companions completed the 300-mile trek in a month. Like Colson, they also struck a wet season, and at one point they had to wade through bogs and knee-deep pools of water. Such conditions made for tough going, but the dramatic upsurge of plants and wildlife within days of the rains enabled the expedition to collect a rich haul, including five species of wrens and chats and 28 species of spiders, 14 of which were new to science.

Madigan found that the Simpson's most common and most conspicuous inhabitants were lizards. But although I kept a sharp lookout, it was some time before I met up with one. Clambering to the crest of yet another dune, I was about to flop down and rest my hot, aching feet

A dusky grass-wren, furtive inhabitant of central Australia's rocky, spinifex-covered hillsides, ventures on to a sandstone slab in search of seeds and insects. When threatened by danger, the grass-wren will run off through the spinifex rather than fly away. The plant's spiky leaves and its own agility protect the bird from predators.

when I noticed a flurry of movement just below the brow of the ridge. A military dragon raced away and disappeared among the spinifex. Its distinctive black and red colouring were reminiscent of a Napoleonic guardsman. This specimen belongs to the group of lizards known as agamids, of which the Australian members are called dragons on account of their spiny ugliness and fearsome threat displays.

The dragons range in size from a few inches to more than three feet. Some possess frills and ruffs that can be erected to scare off attackers; others are encased in thick body armour; and many of them, including the military dragon, are lightning quick in their movements. Most dragons are territorial, and competing males can be be magnificently comic in their territorial displays, dashing around each other on their hind legs and bobbing their heads like absurd mannequins.

Because lizards have no internal mechanism for regulating their temperature, their body heat depends almost entirely on the temperature of their surroundings. But by moving back and forth from sun to shade, or going underground, they are able to keep their body heat within tolerable limits. One 19th-Century naturalist described the fate of a luckless blue-tongue skink that found itself without shelter on the Simpson sands. "Having my hands full of specimens," he wrote, "I asked a blackfellow to look after it and not to let it escape, when to my surprise he simply put it down on the hot sand. It was perfectly alive when he put it down, having been captured in its hole, and when placed on the ground it began to travel at some rate, but after going five yards its movements became slower and slower, and before ten yards had been traversed, they ceased and the animal was quite dead—simply apparently baked to death by contact with the hot sand."

Most lizards rely on a diet of insects, which provides them not only with food but also with moisture. Ants, for example, have a high water content, and one three-inch lizard might easily consume 700 ants in a day. Many species also store moisture in their skins or body tissue, enabling them to survive drought. Some dragons have been known to last for 80 days without drinking, and one small nocturnal gecko can live for a year on the food and moisture stored in its body.

Hoping to see more of the Simpson's wildlife, I got to my feet again and stumbled down the far side of the dune in the wake of the military dragon. As I reached the bottom, I noticed the cup-like nest of a grass-wren in one of the spinifex clumps. Its owners, however, were mere flecks of colour as they flitted through the surrounding tussocks, pecking at seeds and insects as they went. Grass-wrens are so elusive that some species are probably still undiscovered. Even sightings of some known species are astonishingly rare. The Eyrean grass-wren, first found at Lake Eyre in 1874, was not spotted again until 1961; and the black grass-wren of the Kimberley Mountains in Western Australia escaped new detection for 60 years until its rediscovery by a British Museum expedition in 1969.

Even more elusive than the grass-wrens is the night or spinifex parrot, a mottled green, yellow and dark brown bird about ten inches long. The last specimen was caught in 1912, although there have been tantalizing reports of more recent sightings. Some ornithologists argue that the night parrot still inhabits the Simpson, but sporadic daytime expeditions have failed to flush the bird into the open; and the Simpson is a difficult place to work at night. Early observers reported that the night parrot nests inside the spinifex clumps, laying up to four eggs in a cavity that it reaches by way of a tunnel through the grass. So far as is known, it feeds off the seeds lying near its snug retreat, creeping out at night to fly to the nearest water, which may be many miles away. On its return flight, the bird skims low as it heads back into cover, making a right-angled turn on landing. The Aborigines call the parrot *myrr-lumbing*, a word meant to imitate both its whistling cry and the frog-like croak it makes when startled.

Roasting as I was in the heat of noon, I found it difficult to conceive of the Simpson cooling off at night. But temperatures can drop so low that many desert birds become torpid. The real threat to them, however, is not the cold, but—as for all other animal life—the daytime's intense heat. Reproduction in such a harsh environment brings its own problems for the birds. Favourable nesting conditions are most likely to occur when rain falls, insects and other food species breed, and the desert blooms. But in the Simpson, rainfall is not predictable, so many birds have acquired the ability to begin their breeding cycle at almost a moment's notice. The speed with which some of them rush to breed has become something of a joke among Australian ornithologists. The black-faced wood-swallow, for example, starts courting as soon as the first raindrops fall; and one tongue-in-cheek naturalist has declared that the bird starts to gather nesting material whenever it sees a cloud.

By now the temperature was well above 100° F., and I decided it was time to retrace my footsteps. As I toiled up the dune overlooking the airstrip, I suddenly realized that I was being watched. A yellow dingo, ears pricked, was standing on the crest gazing down at me. We stared at each other for a full minute and then I started climbing as quickly as possible, keen to get closer to this wild dog, the supreme Australian predator. By the time I reached the top, however, the only signs of the dingo were the tracks it had left in the red sand.

For a long while I stood looking back over the landscape. "Before ever the mushroom growth of the human race had sprung up," wrote C. T. Madigan, "countless millions of suns had arisen, shone upon the great desert disc of the interior, just as it is today, and sunk back in a blaze of red." The scene had the same awe-inspiring impact on me. Turning, I trudged down the dune back to the comfort and safety of the aeroplane, the bell-like sound of bird song ringing once again in my ears.

Lizards on the Defensive

More than 240 lizard species are found in Australia, many of them in the Outback. Their survival stems largely from their resistance to drought, but is also due in no small measure to their ability to defend themselves against such predators as eagles, snakes, dingoes, carnivorous marsupials—and one another.

The lizards combat predators with a remarkable variety of defence mechanisms and life-saving stratagems. Some species are armed with dangerous weapons: Gould's sand goanna (right) is a five-foot-long flesh-eater with sharp-toothed jaws, raking claws and a whip-lash tail. Others, less well-equipped for a violent showdown, resort to bluff as a defence. The threat displays of these lizards—enhanced in some cases by weird appendages that can be deployed to give an impression of ferocity—are effective as well as bizarre.

The outstanding bluffers are the bearded dragon and frilled lizard, which take their names from the curious folds of skin that surround their heads. The bearded dragon, a stoutly built insect-eater, rarely has to run away from danger; instead it assumes a challenging stance and intimidates predators by puffing out its spiky jaw-fringe. If this frightening deceit fails, it may escape with a short burst of speed.

The frilled lizard, by contrast, is a fleet-footed species that dashes for cover when in danger. If cornered, however, it turns on its foe and suddenly unfurls its colourful, umbrella-like frill, startling the pursuer while it makes good its escape.

Both of these species accentuate their back-to-the-wall behaviour by hissing violently and opening their jaws wide—ruses employed by many other Outback lizards, including the blue-tongue skink and shingleback. These actions draw the attention of predators to the lizards' tongues, which are coloured an alarmingly vivid blue.

The thorny devil, a relative of the frilled lizard, has a more passive method of self-defence. It lacks weapons and employs no shock tactics; but it is protected by a thick skin bristling with spines. If its appearance fails to deter predators, the thorny devil simply puts its head down and weathers the attack. Usually its armour proves impregnable and, once the attacker has given up, the thorny devil returns to the tasks that occupy most of its time—catching and eating the 1,000 to 5,000 ants it needs each day to survive.

A Gould's sand goanna meets threat with threat by adopting an aggressive pose. Emphasizing its size by standing erect and puffing out its conspicuous throat skin, this powerful lizard carries an explicit warning in its splayed claws. Should an adversary ignore the danger signals, the goanna will attack, using teeth, claws and tail as offensive weapons.

Surprised in the open, a centralian blue-tongue skink (left) tries to trick its way out of danger by inflating its body to give a disconcerting impression of size. In spite of its cumbersome appearance and feeble-looking limbs, this 18-inch lizard can make a speedy dash to safety if its bluff fails.

Standing squarely on its bulldog-like limbs, a shingleback (above) creates an impression of ferocity by threatening with its open mouth and conspicuous blue tongue. Ironically, the teeth of this lizard are used mainly for crunching up the fruits, flowers, insects and molluscs on which it feeds.

Hissing violently, its jaws opening, a bearded dragon (above) tries to intimidate an enemy with the bristling frill around its mouth. The species, otherwise helpless, uses its camouflage colouring to avoid hostile encounters.

A frilled lizard's ruff explodes, framing its gaping mouth (right). The startling frill is supported on bony ribs that run from the back of the creature's mouth, so that the dimensions of the frill depend on how wide the mouth is opened.

In spite of its grotesque appearance, which has earned it the scientific name Moloch horridus, a thorny devil presents a danger only to the ants on which it feeds. Too sluggish to outpace most predators, the eight-and-a-half-inch-long lizard stands its ground and defends itself by hiding its head between its armoured forelimbs. The spiky lump on its neck, perhaps being mistaken for its head, then bears the brunt of any attack.

3/ A Dogged Survivor

My men saw two or three beasts like hungry wolves, lean like so many skeletons.

CAPT. WILLIAM DAMPIER/ *A VOYAGE TO NEW HOLLAND IN THE YEAR 1699*

When my father was a boy living on a small farm in coastal New South Wales, he often heard dingoes howling as he stood at night guarding the family cornfield from marauding animals. Although he was aware that these wild dogs—the largest of Australia's land predators—would not hurt him, their mournful chorus prickled his skin and made him clutch his shotgun a little tighter, while the sheepdogs that shared his vigils whined uneasily, hackles bristling. I myself was a man before I heard my first dingo; they have been all but wiped out along Australia's south-eastern seaboard—shot, trapped, or poisoned by strychnine and by "1080" (sodium mono fluoro-acetate) dropped in bait from aeroplanes. Pockets of dingoes survive there, as they do in many settled parts of Australia, but continual persecution has forced them to become solitary, fugitive beasts, and their wild blood has been diluted through inter-breeding with domestic dogs.

Not until I travelled to the lonely places of the Centre did I see dingoes in their true wild state. In the dark gorges of ancient mountain ranges and out on the lonely wastes of the deserts dingoes still thrive, and it was there that I began to piece together a picture of their way of life. At night among the desert sand dunes I often heard their high-pitched, blood-tingling calls as I sat by a dying campfire or lay huddled in my sleeping bag. Camped one evening on the fringe of the Simpson Desert, I looked up from the meal I was cooking to see the glowing eyes of a dingo beyond the firelight. So contemptuous was it of human interlopers that, when I awoke next morning, I saw from its tracks that it had walked only a few feet from where I had been sleeping.

Later that day I had the closest glimpse I have ever had of a dingo. I was searching for lizards along a dry gully when I looked up to see one of the wild dogs on a dune above me, not more than 50 yards away. There was no breeze to betray my scent and the dingo did not sense my presence. It began moving down the dune towards me and I crouched behind a clump of spinfex to watch it. The dingo was hunting, travelling slowly over the sand with its nose down and shortish, brush-like tail held high. From its size I guessed it was a male—a full-grown specimen standing about 20 inches high at the shoulder and weighing perhaps 35 pounds. It was pale beige-yellow, with lighter undersides and a white chest. I imagine that from a distance it could have been mistaken for a domestic dog, but I was close enough to recognize the characteristic dingo features: a chunky head with powerful jaws, and short, triangular, permanently cocked ears. I even caught a glimpse of its alert almond eyes; but then it must have spotted me because it turned and ran back up the dune, pausing for a second to look back before it vanished over the crest.

While I was travelling through the Outback, a team of zoologists from the Commonwealth Scientific and Industrial Research Organization (CSIRO) was coming to the end of a ten-year study of the dingo in the arid Centre and the wetter eastern Highlands. The CSIRO programme was financed mainly by the Australian Meat Research Committee, which was alarmed about the slaughter of livestock by dingoes and by the ineffectiveness of traditional methods of control. Various attempts have been made to exterminate the dingo where it is a menace—shooting, trapping, poisoning and even the construction of a 6,000-mile dog-proof fence around the dingo's Outback stronghold—but none has had any great success. Working on the philosophy that it is best to "know thine enemy", the zoologists set out to investigate the dingo's biology, numbers, movements, predatory habits and social behaviour. From their findings there emerges a fascinating portrait of Australia's wild dog—a mainly solitary hunter than can band into packs to bring down large animals, a blood-thirsty slayer of livestock that tends its young with devotion, a creature so well-adapted for life in the arid interior that it has withstood more than a century of intense persecution.

Among the investigators based in the Centre was Laurie Corbett, a zoologist who had already devoted ten years to gathering information on the dingo. He spent much of this time in the field—observing the animals from hides constructed near waterholes, watching breeding families at their dens, and monitoring their movements with the aid of tiny radio transmitters he managed to attach to their necks. By the time Laurie concluded his work, some of the dingoes in his study area had grown so used to him that they sometimes invaded his camp to scavenge for scraps and even allowed him to follow them over the dunes when they went hunting.

In the Harts Mountains of the Macdonnell Ranges, about 80 miles north-east of Alice Springs, Laurie and other members of the CSIRO research team gained an insight into dingo family life by watching an occupied den on moonlit nights over a period of three months. Dingoes breed once a year, in the autumn, and their pups are born in late winter or early spring, usually in excavated rabbit warrens or caves. This particular den, in a rabbit warren by a dry riverbed, contained five pups—an average litter. The watchers were surprised to find four dingoes attending the young: the father, the mother and a pair of non-breeding yearlings—one male and one female. Only the two bitches fed the pups; the males seemed to act purely as hunters and guardians.

The pups were left alone all day and at first they stayed deep within their burrow. After about four weeks, when their legs were strong enough to carry them short distances, they wandered away from the den each morning and made separate "camps" farther along the riverbed. Each evening, however, they trotted back to the den and waited for their elders to return from their daytime resting places, then greeted them boisterously. After about half an hour at the den, the adult dingoes set off again into the night to hunt for rabbits. Since rabbits were introduced into Australia in the early 19th Century, they have gradually replaced small marsupials like bandicoots, rat-kangaroos and hare-wallabies as the main item of the dingo diet in the Centre.

Rabbits were plentiful near the den, but the adult dingoes ignored them and vanished to hunt farther afield; the "local" rabbits were left as game for the pups, which were coached in the art of stalking by the younger bitch. The pups learned quickly, so that when they were about six months old and almost fully grown, they were abandoned by their parents and thrown on their own resources. Four months later, however, one of the pups was frequently seen with an adult male, following its every move; the observation suggests that, after leaving their parents, young dingoes refine their hunting techniques by imitating their elders.

A clay-pan, surrendering its surface moisture to the dessicating Outback sun, supplies scant moisture to clumps of desert cane grass.

The den was more than a mile from the nearest water and the investigators were at first at a loss to explain how the pups obtained water during the period after weaning when they still did not stray from home. They knew that adult dingoes derive some water from the carcasses of their prey, and that they drink when they can—up to three pints a day. One hot evening the members of the team solved the puzzle. The mother trotted back from the pool and the pups approached her quietly—not falling over each other and snapping excitedly as they did when she brought them food. They began licking at her mouth and the observers realized that she was regurgitating water for her pups.

The scientists also kept watch over three other dens located on Mount Dare, the lonely cattle station where I had searched for the desert hardyhead. The area was stricken by drought; there were no near-by rabbit warrens to provide easy pickings and other game was scarce. The adult dingoes solved the food problem by leading their month-old pups about the countryside and giving them large grasshoppers to eat. When they had exhausted the supplies of insects in one area, they moved to another. Later, when the pups were about six weeks old, their mothers split the litters into smaller groups which they placed in separate dens. Two litters eventually became mingled, and it is likely that both bitches combined efforts to feed their joint offspring.

Sometimes dingoes work together for more bloody purposes, as when they band together to hunt large animals that one alone could not kill. Dingo packs are sometimes six or seven strong, especially before the breeding season when a bitch may team up with several rival suitors, and their hunting methods are as efficient as a well-rehearsed military manoeuvre. These large packs are a serious menace to livestock. When they find a herd of cattle, they deploy their forces in a series of mock attacks, going first for the calves and then, when the mothers rush to the aid of their young, turning their attention to the cows. These tactics distract the cows long enough for a single dingo to slink behind them and slaughter a calf. Then the pack runs off and waits some distance away until the cows have collected their calves and ambled off. If the dead calf's mother stands guard, the dingoes will wait patiently—for days if necessary—until she abandons the carcass. The pack then returns to feast at leisure.

Occasionally, dingoes join forces to hunt red kangaroos. An Outback bushman who had seen such a spectacle as a young man described it to Eric Rolls, author of *They All Ran Wild*, an account of animal pests in

Two dingo pups, part of a litter of five, huddle together at the entrance to the family den. As soon as the three-week-old pups are sturdy enough, they will set up daytime resting places away from the den. By the time they are six months old, and almost fully grown, the pups will be abandoned by their parents to hunt on their own.

Australia. The bushman was out hunting with his father when a big red 'roo bounded desperately over a sandhill with a creamy, bitch dingo hard on its heels and five dogs strung out in a line behind her. The bitch forced the kangaroo to turn and stand at bay, bolt upright against a tree, until the rest of the pack caught up and joined the fray, snarling and yelping. One dog worked its way behind the kangaroo and bit the butt of its tail, then two more leapt in and tore at its rump. Bloodied and frantic, the kangaroo made a bid to escape, "hopping a bit lopsided", reported the bushman, who was watching the black drama through the telescopic sight of his rifle. The pack was gaining on the injured 'roo, but the bushman did not wait to see the outcome of the hunt; at a range of about 200 yards he shot the bitch. Her retinue fled, but the two men began to call them, imitating the dingo howl. One dingo answered from 500 yards away and they lured it to within 300 yards. There it stopped, too nervous to approach any closer. The bushman's father shot the dingo where it stood.

Large packs of dingoes are found only in remote parts of the Outback such as the Centre, where the wild dogs are comparatively free from disturbance by man. Even there a pack of six is an uncommon sight. Of a thousand animals seen by the CSIRO team over a period of eight years, 73 per cent were solitary and less than 10 per cent were in groups of three or more. In the Outback, where long droughts alternate with brief periods of plenty, the populations of prey species fluctuate and the social behaviour of the dingoes changes accordingly. When animals like rabbits and red kangaroos are numerous, the dingoes may be seen hunting them down in packs, but during droughts, when prey is scarce, the wild dogs go their own ways, or maintain their association in the form of loose-knit "tribes" of as few as three dogs that share a single territory but hunt separately.

One cool morning in the Centre, Laurie and another observer watched one of these tribes in operation. For three hours they followed a large male, a smaller male and a bitch in season as they made a hunting foray through their shared territory. At first the animals hunted together for rabbits and lizards, the larger male showing his dominant status by chasing the bitch off a rabbit carcass. The bitch eventually caught another rabbit and disappeared with it, while the two males trotted together for half a mile before the larger animal lay down among some rocks to rest. The other male wandered off to hunt lizards on his own. For a time the landscape was hushed, apparently lifeless. About half an hour later the large male suddenly howled and trotted to a ledge overlooking the route he had travelled. He lay watching intently until the female came into sight, then he sprang up and ran back to meet her. They greeted each other by licking faces and then trotted to another ledge where the bitch lay down to rest. The male did not stay with her; he vanished over a ridge, presumably to continue his hunting alone. Although less spectacular than the bushman's account of the dingo pack running down the kangaroo, these observations are more typical of the way in which dingo society operates.

Although the fluctuating food resources of the Outback compel dingoes to be mainly solitary, they can communicate with each other at distances of up to several miles. At night they maintain contact mainly by sound, relying on a wide range of calls to relay "messages". Howling, which is most intense in the breeding season, is the commonest call. Dingoes utter three basic kinds of howl—a long drawn-out note, a quavering call and an abrupt howl—with many variations. Although the meaning of each sound is unknown, some are apparently used to attract mates, some to locate fellow hunters, and others to call pups to a kill. Howling also serves to warn other dingoes off a territory.

In addition to howling, dingoes utter a sound that Laurie described as a "bark howl"—a call that begins with one or more barks like those made by a domestic dog and trails off into a wavering howl. The cry is probably uttered to warn pups of danger; the CSIRO team heard it most frequently when dingoes detected their presence near occupied dens. Yet another sound in the dingo's repertoire of calls is a moaning cry that is usually made when the dogs approach a waterhole. It is probably a signal to warn dingoes that are already at a waterhole that the newcomers wish to come and drink.

The scarce waterholes of the arid interior are usually shared by several rival dingo packs, tribes, families or individuals—and are often the centre of disputes. Precedence at the waterholes is sometimes decided by which dingo or group of dingoes sees the other first. If a dingo coming towards the pool spots another dingo already drinking, it may stop and wait some distance away until the waterhole is left vacant. Alternatively, if the approaching dingo is seen first, the dog that is drinking at the hole may speedily depart.

Because waterholes often mark the boundaries of adjacent territories, the wild dogs are understandably wary when they approach them. Laurie hid in a hide to obtain a bird's eye view of relations at a waterhole shared by two packs. On one occasion he saw a pack of seven animals cautiously approach the water, from which another pack had recently departed. The new arrivals came to within a hundred yards of the pool, then waited to make sure no others were around. After several minutes one of the dogs, the leader, trotted towards the pool to reconnoitre, tail raised high and hackles on end. The other dingoes in his pack followed quietly in a compact group; but when they neared the water's edge, they abandoned their air of caution. Full of bravado, they began throwing up dust, making playful attacks on one another—acting like "a bunch of Hell's Angels hitting town on Saturday night", as Laurie described the scene.

A few minutes later Laurie found out how the same pack of dingoes treated an interloper that encroached on its territory—in this case, himself. After watching the dingoes head away from the pool, he climbed from his hide intending to follow a pack member. He had not gone far when he realized that the rest of the pack was approaching him. Within seconds he was surrounded by seven aggressive, self-confident dingoes. Although Laurie knew that recorded dingo attacks on humans have been made only by provoked animals—those caught in traps or kept in captivity—he was worried. The dingoes walked stiff-legged around him, gingerly sniffing him, their fur bristling menacingly. Laurie froze, not daring to move a muscle while the dingoes conducted their examination. Eventually they moved away—only to catch up with him again and repeat the performance. Once more Laurie was subjected to their nerve-wracking examination before, satisfied that he was neither a rival dingo nor a potential meal, they loped off.

A dingo from a rival group would have fared worse. Disputes between the wild dogs are not always settled amicably, and dingoes that encroach on others' territory often come into conflict. Males competing for a mate often fight, too, as the scarred heads of many of them testify. Nor is aggressive behaviour confined to rival packs or amorous males: within each pack, tribe or family there is a strict hierarchy—a "pecking order" that is enforced by a strict code of behaviour. The dominant animals within the groups have self-confident postures, often carry their tails high and take precedence over others at a carcass. The subservient animals reveal their lowly position by cringing, flattening their ears and by licking the mouths of the dominant beasts.

Dingoes are reputed to travel great distances in search of prey; but by tracing the movements of more than a hundred dingoes, the CSIRO team found that the wild dogs spend most of their lives within a three-or-four-mile radius of the same waterhole. Of the dingoes tagged by the scientists only two were seen more than 20 miles from the place where they were captured; and more than 75 per cent did not travel more than four miles. During long droughts, however, dingoes do disperse outwards from their normal range, wandering far and wide in search of food. Unusually heavy rainfalls will also send them farther afield; rain sets many desert animals breeding, thus opening up hitherto barren hunting grounds for the dingoes to exploit. In such periods of plenty, dingoes even venture into the heart of the Simpson Desert, returning gaunt and skeletal to their old haunts after food supplies have been exhausted.

The movements of dingoes are determined not only by the climate and the availability of prey, their range is also prescribed by a man-made barrier: the dingo fence. Three times as long as the Great Wall of China, this 6,000-mile wire boundary snakes from the coast of South Australia to that state's border with New South Wales, then zig-zags far into Queensland before it turns south and ends 150 miles from Queensland's Gold Coast. The fence is a monument to the anxiety that dingoes arouse in sheep and cattle farmers. Each 50-mile stretch of the barrier is patrolled by a boundary rider whose job is to repair damage done by blundering kangaroos or strong desert winds. The fence was designed to contain most of the dingo population to the arid, mostly unfarmed interior. But the state governments also take their fight to the

Barely full-grown but already independent, a gaunt female dingo pads across the Simpson Desert wastes, heading for a near-by waterhole.

enemy; they employ men known as "doggers", either paying them a wage or offering them bounty money for the scalps of dingoes.

The battle between dogger and dingo is not one-sided. The doggers are armed with an arsenal of guns, traps and poisons, and have an intimate knowledge of their quarry's habits; but on their side the wild dogs have remarkable cunning. Dingoes are adept at detecting and avoiding traps, and are quick to sense when a bait is poisoned. The most wily dingoes know when they are being hunted—and by what method—and take the necessary evasive action. Faced with such a difficult quarry, the doggers often earn their bounty money only by resorting to unconventional methods.

Eric Rolls described how one dogger, William Baldwin, of Tibooburra, on the south-eastern corner of the Simpson Desert, caught a bitch dingo that with her mate and pups had been killing sheep. Baldwin succeeded in killing the dog and the pups, but the bitch eluded him. She sprang every hidden trap that Baldwin set by gently pushing her forepaws through the surface covering of sand. The dogger realized that the dingo was following him and springing the traps as he set them. He also noticed that she always trotted along the left-hand tyre mark of his Land Rover. Armed with this insight, he devised a plan to catch her. He dug a hole at a point along the tyre mark, set a trap in it and disguised it with a layer of sand on which he etched the tyre tread with a stick. In due course the dingo reached the hidden trap, did not notice anything suspicious, and was caught.

On another occasion Baldwin exploited the innate curiosity of dingoes to kill a particularly troublesome dog he had been hunting for six months. He was familiar with the trails habitually used by the animal, but every trap he set on them was avoided with contemptuous ease. The dogger tried putting one trap on a trail used by the dingo and other traps on either side of the first one, hoping that the wary beast would step into one while avoiding the others. The dingo simply gave all the traps a wide berth. Baldwin finally reckoned that the only way to catch the dingo was to distract its attention from the ground long enough for the animal to walk unsuspectingly into a trap. He built a miniature windmill out of paper and placed it to one side of the dingo's trail, along which he concealed a trap. It was a clever ploy, but it failed. The contraption was so bizarre that when the dingo spotted the device it simply turned tail and fled. Baldwin tried the idea again, this time substituting a few cockatoo feathers for the windmill—just enough to make the dingo give them a sideways glance as it drew level with the

A kowari, or Byrne's pouched mouse, one of the small animals preyed on by the dingo in the deserts of the Centre, makes its own nocturnal hunting foray for insects, reptiles and small rodents. During the day, this rat-sized, bushy-tailed marsupial escapes the heat by hiding in a deep, cool burrow.

trap. The ruse was successful, and Baldwin collected the bounty money.

Doggers who use poison also resort to unusual stratagems. Laurie heard of one dogger who conducted a running battle with a dingo that studiously avoided his baits. No matter how much the dogger tried to disguise the scent of poison by doctoring his lures with other substances, the dingo always detected the hidden dose of strychnine. Finally, the dogger hit on an unorthodox idea: he poisoned some sweet syrup, placed it in a container in which he cut a small hole, then rode on horseback through the dingo's haunts, dropping blobs of the sticky stuff as he went. The dingo, coming on his pursuer's tracks, fouled its paws in the syrup and stopped to lick it off. The dogger returned later to find the dingo's corpse.

The resourcefulness of dingoes has earned them the grudging respect of the doggers, but stock owners have no sympathy for the species and many would like to see it exterminated. Yet Laurie, while conceding that the interests of farmers and conservationists are difficult to reconcile, thinks that dingoes sometimes actually do cattle owners a service by killing some of their stock. He pointed out that dingoes usually kill calves only during droughts, when the beasts have a poor chance of survival anyway. By killing a calf, Laurie argues, the dingoes unwittingly give its mother a better chance because she no longer has to waste precious grazing by producing milk. Laurie also presents another argument in defence of the wild dog. Large herds of cattle and sheep have destroyed the native vegetation in many parts of the Outback and with it the fauna on which the dingo naturally feeds; as a result of man's tampering with the natural balance, it has been compelled to turn to livestock as a substitute for the diminishing prey species.

Over the large tracts of the Centre where livestock is absent, dingoes still do prey on their traditional quarry—or on rabbits, the introduced substitute. This is also true in isolated parts of their coastal range, as Bob Harden, a research officer with the New South Wales National Parks and Wildlife Service, made clear to me. In his area, Bob told me, dingoes prey on wallabies, bandicoots, possums, mice, brush turkeys, lyre birds—and the ubiquitous rabbit. He admires the dingo in its undisturbed habitat as a creature that has an important role to play in maintaining the natural balance by killing the old, the injured and the diseased animals.

Bob's interest in dingoes goes beyond the strictly professional. "He's a very majestic animal," he told me, "and can be very arrogant around your camp. He'll carry on regardless of the fact that you're there. I'm rather fond of them. I kept two dingoes in my house and they'd only let me and my wife touch our baby." On one occasion, he told me, the domesticated dingoes were asleep on the floor when his 12-month-old son fell down and began to cry. The child's grandfather rose quickly to pick him up, but one of the dingoes moved in front of the baby, growling and barring the grandfather's approach.

Another ranger friend of mine had a more unnerving experience with a captive dingo that he had been in the habit of treating "like a big baby". The dingo, a male, apparently began to resent him for injecting some domesticated dingo bitches with a hormone to prevent them from coming into heat. One day the frustrated dingo suddenly sprang at him with teeth bared. "I knew he'd tear my calves open if I turned to run," the ranger said. "I kicked him and he rolled over for three yards, then sprang at me again. I kicked him over again and then I knew that I had to grab him or I was gone. I fell on him and he bit through my hand—and when a dingo bites, he bites and twists at the same time. I was struggling with my knee on him when fortunately some friends rushed in . . . ."

This incident suggests that the dingo is not easily tamed, yet for thousands of years the Aborigines have maintained a close association with Australia's wild dog. Dingoes feature prominently in Aboriginal folklore. The natives believe, for example, that the Mamu, a mythical dingo, captures and eats the spirit of any child who wanders away from the campfire, and the Aborigines of Cape York have adopted the dingo howl as a lamentation for their dead. Aborigines have also traditionally kept dingoes as companions. As early as 1623 the Dutch explorer Jan Carstenz made a landfall on Australia's north coast and reported that he had seen the tracks of a native accompanied by those of a very large dog; and in the 18th Century James Cook, the celebrated English navigator, noted of the Aborigines, "Tame animals they have none, but dogs."

As recently as 1969, a group of Aborigines who had never before seen a white man were found in the Gibson Desert of Western Australia with 19 skinny, skulking dingoes about their camp. They fondled the dogs but rarely fed them, leaving them to scavenge food from the camp and catch prey themselves. Nor did they use them for hunting, driving them back to camp when they set out on their expeditions. The only practical use the natives made of the dingoes was as "blankets" on freezing desert nights (a "two-dog-night", in Centre parlance, is a very cold one). Elsewhere, Aborigines and dingoes have been found living together in the same kind of rough harmony: nursing Aboriginal women suckle dingo pups at their breasts, but break their legs to prevent them from straying when they are grown.

The relationship between Aborigines and the dingo sheds light on one of the most puzzling aspects of the wild dog: its origins. There are no other wild dogs in Australia, nor are there any indigenous species from which it could have evolved. How, then, did it reach this isolated continent, and when? The absence of dingoes from the island of Tasmania, south of Australia, gives a clue to the date of their arrival. Tasmania was connected to the mainland until 10,000 to 12,000 years ago; if dingoes had colonized Australia before that date, they would probably have spread as far as the island. The earliest accurately dated fossil dingo thus far found is about 3,000 years old; however, others may be 7,000 to 8,000 years old. Accordingly, the dingo must have found its way into Australia not long before that—some time between 8,000 and 12,000 years ago; and it probably arrived by means of an "assisted" sea-passage: brought over from Asia by an influx of Aboriginal tribes.

Its place of origin and ancestral type are more obscure, but Laurie Corbett, along with other experts, has compared dingo skulls with those of other wild dogs and found striking similarities between the dingo and the Indian wolf. If Laurie is correct, then the wild dingoes I saw roaming the Centre may very well be related to the half-wild dogs, called pariahs, of the Middle East and the southern Mediterranean countries, for they too are thought to be descended from the Indian wolf.

In spite of concentrated efforts to eliminate this "newcomer" to Australia, zoologists do not think there is any likelihood of its extinction, at least not in the Centre. Nor do the dingo's enemies, the doggers. An Australian journalist once questioned an old dogger on the likely fate of the dingo. He asked the man how many dingos he had killed. "Thousands", the dogger answered. The journalist was impressed. "Thousands?" he exclaimed. "At that rate there soon won't be any left." The dogger rubbed his jaw and thought for a second before replying. "Listen," he said. "I saw a dingo long before I saw a motor car. I grew up knowing dogs better than people. I reckon that when I'm dead, the dingo'll still be there. That animal's learned how to live."

Monuments Sculpted by Nature

Unique among the inhabited continents, Australia has no ancient, man-made monuments to match, say, the Britons' Stonehenge or the cliff dwellings of the North American Indians. But the Outback compensates for this lack with a rich endowment of geological features: natural monuments that inspired both Aborigines and white settlers to give them names befitting their striking configurations.

In spite of their diversity, these landforms have a common origin: over millions of years they have been sculpted by heat, cold, water and wind. And like unsatisfied artists, these forces continue to chisel away at their creations.

The elements focus on the corners of rocks, eating away at them and rounding off sharp edges. Abrupt shifts of temperature cause the surfaces of rocks to expand and contract, and eventually to strip away. This process, called exfoliation, has helped to chamfer granite blocks into the Devil's Marbles—a jumble of spheroidal boulders north of Alice Springs—and it has been instrumental in rounding the domes of the Olgas (opposite).

As surface layers are worn away, relieving pressure within, great portions of underlying rock may separate along joints and eventually shear off completely. A striking example of this process, called unloading, is the Kangaroo Tail, a 500-foot-long slab of sandstone that has partially split from Ayers Rock.

Water plays a surprisingly important role in carving the arid Outback's landforms. After rain, streams nibble away soft rock, gradually exposing more resistant layers. In this way the quartzite columns of the Organ Pipes were bared in a gorge of the Macdonnell Ranges. On parts of Ayers Rock, water has leached away chemicals that bind the sandstone together, enabling the wind to gouge out the Brain, a complex of tiny caves and pits.

Underground, water has a subtler effect. It combines with decaying organic matter to form mild acids that slowly dissolve buried rocks. In Western Australia this type of weathering has scalloped a once-buried outcrop of granite into Wave Rock, a 50-foot-high overhang that resembles a petrified breaker.

Wind, too, acts as a shaping force. Carrying sand particles that abrade surfaces already weakened by the other elements, it smoothes the Outback's gallery of sculptures.

The Valley of the Mice Women, which draws its name from Aboriginal mythology, is a narrow cleft between two rounded domes of the Olgas. The sides of the domes are pocked by rows of caves dug by rain and wind in a soft layer of sandstone. The gentle, debris-strewn slope at the base is colonized by spinifex and dwarf acacias.

A network of shallow cavities in the hard sandstone crust of Ayers Rock makes an intricate pattern called the Brain (above). Ayers Rock was first infiltrated and weakened by water; then wind, frost and the rotting effect of moisture continued the pitting process.

The jagged cliffs of the Organ Pipes (right) jut in stony ranks in Glen Helen—a gorge cut by the Finke river in the Macdonnell Ranges. The upright, quartzite beds were exposed as the Finke slowly cut down through less resistant layers of sandstone.

A ribbon of sky shows between Ayers Rock and the 500-foot-long, partly detached strip of rock known as the Kangaroo Tail. As surface rock was weathered away, long joints opened up within the main sandstone mass, partly dislodging the slab, and causing other massive pieces to break away and tumble to the base of the Rock.

The Devil's Marbles, 250 miles north of Alice Springs, are a bold example of the shaping force of exfoliation: the peeling away of a rock's surface layers. Masses of granite blocks have been split by the elements along their well-defined lines of weakness (above). As these blocks become detached, heat, cold and water will strip them down into rounded boulders like those on the right, which are strewn across a valley as if they were the playthings of giants.

Resembling a curling breaker, Wave Rock towers over a scrubby plain on the Outback's south-western fringe. The 50-foot-high granite outcrop was once partly buried. Weak organic acids in the soil ate away the rock's underside; then the soil was washed away, revealing the outcrop's concave profile. Where rain has run down the Wave, it has reacted with chemicals in the rock, staining parts of it black.

4/ Secret Worlds of the Macdonnells

For half a mile this gorge, which is nothing more than a zig-zag cleft, cuts its way right through the range. Its narrow bed is filled with water, deep and intensely cold. . . .

BALDWIN SPENCER/ *HORN SCIENTIFIC EXPEDITION TO CENTRAL AUSTRALIA*

Late one afternoon, deep in the lonely Macdonnell Ranges of the Centre, I drove with my party down a dusty track and stopped under the shadowy ramparts of Serpentine Gorge, which cuts into the mountains about 60 miles west of Alice Springs. After the simmering, pitiless heat of the Simpson Desert, now more than 200 miles away to the south-east, this narrow gorge presented a more refreshing challenge. Only the day before, a ranger had told me about a species of fern he thought was new to science and which he had recently discovered clinging high on a cliff in the gorge. Now dusk was falling and the safe, suburban thing to do would have been to wait until morning to explore the gloomy chasm; but my interest had been aroused by mention of the fern, and impulsively I decided to push on into the gorge in an attempt to find it.

We brushed through a clump of bushes growing at the base of towering red walls. The electric buzz of cicadas pierced the gathering darkness, and sticks snapped in the undergrowth as secretive animals retreated at our approach. Suddenly we emerged on to a tiny beach at the edge of a still, silvery-dark pool set between sheer cliffs, with no way round it. A sense of mystery tingled over the pool and in the gorge on the far side. We changed into our swimming costumes, waded neck-deep through the water and scrambled out on to a dry riverbed strewn with big boulders that flash-floods had tumbled like pebbles and in receding had bearded with grey débris. Wallabies, startled by this rare intrusion into their water-locked world, bounded away among the glimmering white trunks of ghost gums. The cicadas fell silent.

It was so beautiful, so peaceful in the gorge that we were drawn on into unknown territory in spite of the impending nightfall. We stumbled along the banks of the riverbed for about half a mile, thrusting through bushes on tracks that the wallabies had beaten on their journeys to water. Eventually we broke through to the edge of a second and much larger pool, its surface darkening as the sun's rays withdrew up the surrounding cliffs. On the far side was a rift in the ranges through which water flowed into the pool: a gash only about six feet wide, with walls rising vertically to nearly 200 feet. It offered the only way forward, so I slipped into the water again and swam towards the opening. Betty, ignoring my yell to stay behind, followed and Dominic swam after her. Only Alison hung back on the dark bank, her expression full of misgivings. Perhaps she had cause to worry about our safety, but the lure of that tiny cleft and the world it guarded was too strong.

We wriggled like pale fish through the dim fissure, not knowing how long it was or what lay ahead. It was an experience both exhilarating and frightening; the walls on each side of us were too steep and slippery to offer any escape if we were to get into difficulties, and scores of little brown bats flitted eerily over our heads. The childhood excitement of spooky fairground grottos had suddenly assumed a thrilling reality.

About 50 yards on, a huge mass of boulders loomed at the end of the fissure and we hauled ourselves over them into the inner gorge, which curved away into shadow. As our eyes adjusted to the gloom, we saw before us the mute survivors of a past age: ancient, palm-like cycads flourishing on the red, stony ground beneath the cliffs. Although there was no sign of the fern we were seeking, these cycads—specimens of *Macrozamia macdonnellii*—were a find just as exciting. With thick, tuberous stems topped with a crown of large, divided leaves, the cycads are the most primitive of all the seed-producing plants—the connecting links between the spore-producing ferns that evolved nearly 400 million years ago and the later flowering plants that fanned across the globe in the Cretaceous Period.

Cycads are among the most long-lived of plants; these specimens had survived in the cool isolation of Serpentine Gorge for at least 500, perhaps a thousand years—while outside, the panoply of history unrolled; while the Byzantine Empire crumbled and the Crusaders clattered against Constantinople; while the Renaissance flowered in Italy and Columbus sailed into the history books. We reached out and touched them tentatively, feeling as if the contact completed a circuit bridging the thousands of years since the Centre was a green and fertile place. And then, in minutes, the darkness closed in, forcing us to grope back over the rocks and swim and stumble down the gorge.

Serpentine is one of several gorges we explored in the western part of the Macdonnell Ranges, the longest and highest chain of mountains in central Australia. Sweeping east and west of Alice Springs in an arc more than 200 miles long, the Macdonnells consist of a series of parallel ridges separated from each other north and south by broad, corridor-like valleys. Although the average height of the mountain ridges is barely 3,000 feet and the highest peak, Mount Liebig, reaches only 5,000 feet, the Macdonnells contain the most remarkable natural architecture in the Centre. Water, wind, sun—and time—have scoured away rock to lay open for inspection the sandwich-layer structure of the mountains, and carved the ridges into a roller-coaster succession of dips and humps. In places, rivers have cut through the ridges from north to south, forming deep, shadowy gorges—such as Serpentine. These gorges are the main attractions of the Ranges, but although they have many visitors each year, they enfold much that is hidden and wild.

My own interest in the gorges had been sparked when I read the journals of the Horn Scientific Expedition, which travelled to the Macdonnells in 1894, hoping to find species that had survived when the rest of inland Australia dried up: giant marsupials, perhaps, or forests of deciduous trees. The expedition's wilder hopes were not fulfilled, but it did find repositories of the continent's past: moist, rock-bound refuges of water-dependent ferns, cycads, insects and other invertebrates found nowhere else in the arid Centre. The gorges of the Macdonnells are secret worlds that I had long wanted to visit, since to enter them is to step back to an age when the heart of Australia was verdant.

To reach the ranges we had flown 300 miles north from Oodnadatta. Our journey took us over a desert plain studded with flat-topped mesas, the weathered remnants of an ancient tableland. The mesas are capped with singularly hard and resistant layers of laterite rock, and record the tableland's level before the land surface was cut down by ancient rivers. For much of the journey we followed the winding course of the Centre's longest surviving river, the Finke, whose network of dry flood-channels patterned the earth in places like an electrical circuit diagram. The Finke once flowed more than a thousand miles, but now it peters out only about 400 miles from its source in the Macdonnells, on the south-western edge of the Simpson. On the way to its death, the Finke passes

Simpson's Gap slices through a mountain ridge in the Macdonnell Ranges of central Australia. The narrow gorge was formed over a span of millions of years by streams which cut down through the banded rock layers of the ridge. The bed of the present stream, along which river red gums cluster, fills after occasional heavy rains and the rushing floodwaters continue the process of erosion.

close to a stony or so-called gibber desert, and we saw it down below—a hideous wasteland of small, purple-red stones glistening in coats of iron oxides. I was glad when this inert, almost sterile landscape fell away behind us, and the southernmost ridges of the Macdonnells loomed ahead.

We made our base in the small town of Alice Springs, which straddles the wide bed of the Todd river where it has cut a broad gap in the ranges. The town is an oasis of trees and gardens that draws its water from an artesian water table *beneath* the sandy gravel bed of the Todd; the river seldom flows through Alice more than two or three times each year, and then usually for only a few days each time. Inured to long droughts, the townspeople hold an annual "Henley-on-Todd Regatta"—running along the dry river-bed with their feet protruding from the bottom of replicas of yachts. Aborigines camp under gum trees in "mid-stream" without getting their feet wet. Only rainfalls of two inches or more send water licking down from the Macdonnells into the cracked channels that fissure the desert plain.

Much of this moisture quickly evaporates or sinks into the river-beds, but some pools and waterholes remain long after the streams run dry. Clear water can be found in rock basins in the foothills above the grey-green, splotched floor of the desert, or in chains of waterholes in the creek-beds, or deep under the parched river sand, where you have to dig for it. In rare places, where mineral-rich artesian water seeps under pressure to the surface, mound springs may form; the minerals are precipitated from the water and build up walls, against which desert sand accumulates. I had seen glittering, soda encrusted mound springs at Dalhousie Springs, but near Alice Springs some had been colonized by plants and the water seeped through their rush-choked sides or welled up in small pools amid clusters of nutgrass.

All these sources of water are sustainers of life in the Centre, but only in the Macdonnells are there large, permanent pools. They do not dry up because they lie in gorges so deep and narrow that the sun shines on them for only a short time each day—some never receive direct sunlight. Cupped in the rough hands of the mountains, the pools are like magic in the Centre, for around them are moist micro-climates in which live species normally found only in the continent's wetter coastal regions.

I began my exploration of the gorges early one morning, starting with Simpson's Gap, about five miles west of Alice Springs. At first I crunched along the sandy bed of a stream laced with rock pools and strewn with tiny yellow seed cups of river red gums. These trees grew in the middle of the stream bed: handsome giants up to 80 feet high,

A ghost gum branches gracefully from a cliff ledge above Simpson's Gap in the Macdonnell Ranges. The white bark of this eucalypt lends it a spectral appearance from which the tree's name comes. Aborigines rub off the powdery surface of the bark and use it as a pigment with which to paint rocks or daub their bodies for tribal ceremonies.

with mottled grey, white and red trunks that seemed as solid as the rocky ramparts above them. River red gums have two sets of roots—one spreading out horizontally to absorb moisture near the surface, the other penetrating vertically down through the dry soil to tap reservoirs of underground water. The root-systems provide a firm foothold, enabling the trees to resist the frothing brown walls of floodwater that periodically smash down the water-course. On the cliffs, ghost gums grew from tiny crevices, their alpine-snowy trunks anchored by networks of roots that spread over the rock-face, finding support and nourishment in the smallest cracks. Both species of gum tree are eucalypts—trees characterized by their oily, pungent-smelling leaves and the peculiar structure of their flowers. In all eucalypts the petals are fused and form a protective cap around the flower. The cap is forced off when the flower opens, leaving behind the bushy, often colourful stamens as the most conspicuous feature of the eucalypt blossom.

While I was admiring the trees I noticed a delicate little head peeping at me from a jumble of rocks. It was a black-flanked rock-wallaby, and I stared at it for several seconds before I saw four or five more, only ten yards away. Their grey-brown bodies blended perfectly with the boulders, slotting into the landscape, like those hidden shapes in comic-book picture-puzzles. When I moved towards them they dashed off, bounding sure-footedly over the rocks.

On the creek-bed, black columns of ants hurried busily through piles of bacon-crisp eucalyptus bark and blue dragonflies hovered lazily over the rocks. I sat down on a fallen tree-trunk, beneath ferns growing in damp niches in the cliff, and watched a galah, or rose-breasted cockatoo, flying towards its leaf-lined nest in a near-by hollow tree. A sense of peace welled up in me, like clear water rising in a spring; but then a rush of air above me made me look up and I saw the steel-blue form of a peregrine falcon diving headlong on the galah. There was a thud, a puff of feathers, and the lifeless body of the small cockatoo tumbled like a rag doll to the ground. The peregrine—a rare species in the Centre—pulled out of its swoop but, seeing me, did not descend to recover its prey. It flew off down the gorge and was out of sight before the last pink breast feather of its victim had floated to earth.

I walked farther into Simpson's Gap and saw evidence of many geological periods "written" in the stratified walls of its towering bluffs. The Macdonnells are among the most ancient mountains on earth, with foundations of metamorphic rock produced under heat and pressure in Pre-Cambrian times, more than 600 million years ago. These were

Nose to the ground, an echidna shuffles across a patch of red gravel in the Centre. If attacked on hard ground, the animal rolls into a spiny ball to protect itself. On soft soil, however, it retreats into the ground, burrowing with its powerful feet until only its protective back is exposed. Once buried, the echidna splays out its claws and secures an unyielding underground grip.

covered by layer upon layer of conglomerates, quartzites, sandstones, shales and limestones that were deposited during the Cambrian and Ordovican Periods, up to perhaps 400 million years ago. It was then that violent earth movements squeezed the sandwich-layered rock strata from the north and south, crumpling them up into a series of parallel mountain crests that may have attained a height of 15,000 feet. The peaks wore down slowly through the aeons until about 100 million years ago, when the western two-thirds of Australia was uplifted near its present elevation. Rejuvenated rivers then gouged out the soft rocks between the more resistant quartzites of the ridges and finally breached the ridges themselves to produce the present gorges.

Each of the gorges of the Macdonnells has its own character—gorges like Serpentine, where we saw the colony of cycads; and Standley Chasm, some 24 miles west of Simpson's Gap, which sunlight penetrates only for an hour in the middle of the day, making the red rocks glow as if they were lit from within. But perhaps the most fascinating are those created by the Finke river. Flowing south-east from its source in the north-western ranges, the river has cut through each of the ridges in turn, carving Ormiston Gorge near its headwaters, with cliffs banded in purple, white, red and ochre, Glen Helen Gorge farther south and, most bizarre of all, the long Finke Gorge, with its valley of unique cabbage palms. The first of these gorges we visited was Glen Helen.

On the floor of Glen Helen the Finke spreads into a large pool where, the Aborigines believe, the first human surfaced to survey the world. The pool was still when we reached it. A slight breeze barely blunted the edge of the noonday heat and, to cool myself, I waded into the pool and floated on my back. The red walls of the gorge rose above me and a rainbow bird, Australia's representative of the bee-eaters, darted overhead in a flash of brilliant colour, heading, perhaps, for its nesting tunnel in a sandy bank.

Farther downstream were other pools, each with minute wonders to unfold. Red-backed kingfishers perched high in dead trees, eyes beadily alert for insects, and a thorny devil—a grotesquely armoured lizard—flicked its long tongue as it followed a trail of black ants, its spiny skin changing from rich gold to deep red as it blended with the changing background. I found the widely-spaced tracks of hopping mice: rodent mammals that have the appearance and bounding gait of miniature kangaroos. Elsewhere were the tracks of echidnas, but I had little hope of seeing these spiny anteaters; they bury themselves in the sand at the first hint of danger, leaving only their protective backs uncovered.

A lone palm tree, one of many that grace Palm Valley in the Macdonnell Ranges, grows amid a carpet of flowers and shrubs that have sprung up around a pool. The palms, found nowhere else in Australia, are believed to be the descendants of trees that grew here millions of years ago on the edge of an inland sea.

Some of the pools in Glen Helen are nearly a hundred feet deep: fountains of life that harbour small fish, crustaceans and frogs. I found them ringed by reeds, the rocks on their margins covered with moss that provided a habitat for earthworms and snails found only here and on the continent's coastal fringes. Budgerigars, finches and rainbow birds flicked around the pools, while white-faced herons stalked fish in the shallows and little pied cormorants, resembling long-necked penguins, perched on dead branches above them. Occasionally, grey fantails hawked for insects near the surface of the water and, once, a flock of red-tailed cockatoos swept in to drink, shrieking raucously. Everywhere in this fertile heart of an arid land, I found ferns thriving in moist niches; sprouting from damp cracks in the cliffs above the pools, or growing between rocks at the water's edge. Few of these ferns have common names, and their scientific names—such as *Adiantum hispidulum* and *Cyclosorus gongylodes*—give no idea of the beauty of their leaves, which covered the rocks with an intricate green tracery.

The following day brought a fitting end to our stay in the Macdonnells: a visit to the Finke Gorge, one of the largest along the river before it breaks out of the mountains into the desert plain. Within this gorge is Palm Valley, an oasis of cabbage palms, *Livistona mariae*, and yet another refuge of the cycad *Macrozamia*. I had wanted to see the cycads there ever since reading a description of them by the Australian writer, Jeff Carter: "In the shady recesses of the gorge, reflected red light from the stone walls appears to mix with the pale green of cycads to produce an eerie magenta hue . . . In wind they wave like seaweed." But even more exciting than the cycads, as I was to find out, are the palms, which grow nowhere else on the continent.

More than 3,000 of the palms grow along the gorge, about half in Palm Valley itself. They are reputed to be 5,000 years old, but this is wildly wrong: Peter Latz, a botanist with the Department of the Northern Territory, told me the tallest, which reach a height of one hundred feet, are between a hundred and 300 years old. They are, however, unique descendants of palms that graced the shores of an inland sea that lapped the base of the Macdonnells millions of years ago. The palms and cycads are not the only interesting plants growing in the gorge. Springs, pools and seepage areas support almost one-quarter of all the plant species in the Centre—many of them rare and as yet unclassified. Little wonder that I was anxious to spend a day in Palm Valley.

I nearly failed to make it. Ever since arriving in the Macdonnells I had been fighting a fever I had picked up in the Simpson. Only large doses of antibiotics and the prospect of seeing the palms gave me the strength to make the 100-mile trip westwards from Alice Springs. George Rice, a gutsy little Territorian, drove Betty, Dominic and myself to the valley in a battered old vehicle that he used like a moon-machine, bumping it along a dry water-course and climbing up and down low, dry waterfalls. We travelled part of the way along a corridor through the ranges, navigating across a sea of spinifex so yellow that it resembled a wheatfield. We passed stands of cream-flowered bloodwood trees: red-sapped eucalypts that prune themselves in the withering heat of each dry season, dropping branches as well as leaves so that only the trunk and a few leaves on top remain.

We drove on through lavender-grey tufts of mulla-mulla, clumps of yellow billy buttons and bright-green emu bushes. Pink-purple flowered verbine had spread so fast following recent rain that it covered the track in places, and the slopes above us were studded with cypress pines, an Australian species claimed to be a grandfather in the pine family. Like the palms, these trees are survivors of the distant past, but of a distinctly colder period. They stood, perfect cone-shaped "Christmas trees" on the cooler southern slopes of the Macdonnells, needing frost before their seeds could germinate.

Grey teal and black duck floated on pools in the Finke, which George claimed proudly was older than the Nile. "They thought that the Nile was older until they found fossils under it," he boasted. "There are no fossils under the Finke; the rock isn't young enough for that." We reached Palm Valley at last, hoping to cool ourselves in its pools, but we were disappointed, for the sand had soaked up the water between the quarry-like, sandstone terraces of the gorge and only a few soupy pools remained. Our disappointment evaporated, however, when we walked among the palms. They were even more spectacular than I had expected, with tall, slender trunks, each topped with a burst of green fronds, soaring up from clumps of spinifex and stands of slender, bamboo-like reeds. Young palms no more than a foot high grew in clefts along the stony side of the river-bed; and farther along the valley we found cycads growing luxuriantly beneath damp moss and fern-covered overhangs. A breeze blew along the cliffs, bending the palms and making the whole scene sway gently, like some dream-image of a desert island.

A Scottish-born explorer, John McDouall Stuart, the first man to reach the geographical centre of Australia, may have passed through this valley in 1861, for he recorded in his diary: "We are camped at a good spring where I have found a remarkable palm tree with light green fronds more than ten feet long." Another explorer, Ernest Giles, also found palms in Finke Gorge in 1872, after a group of Aborigines had threatened him and his men with spears and throwing sticks. "Soon after leaving the natives," he reported, "we had the gratification of discovering a magnificent specimen of the Fan palm, a species of *Livistona* . . . and now distinguished as the *Maria Palm* . . . . It was a perfectly new botanical feature to me, nor did I expect to meet it in this latitude." The Horn Scientific Expedition, which visited the valley in 1894, took the first photograph of the palms. Baldwin Spencer, the expedition's zoologist, wrote that it was "rather like sacrilege to touch the trees", but that did not prevent him cutting down a specimen to see if its leaves harboured any new species of insect.

I sat down to rest at the base of a palm, nursing the fever that burned fiercely in my head. While I closed my eyes in the shade of the tree, Betty wandered off up the gorge and scribbled notes, striving to catch in words the vividly contrasting moods of this unlikely valley. Here is what she wrote:

"The whole place is crazy, like a mix-up of Hollywood movies. Little clumps of tropical palms out of a Carmen Miranda musical grow incongruously beside beautiful white ghost gums and light green bamboos. Black crows call in the palm trees, and a dark chocolate goanna twines itself prettily around a stump. There are patches of bitter, skull-sized melons that would make you sick if you could stomach their taste. On the cliffs are the salty white wakes of old waterfalls, looking like giant streaks of bird-lime on the red rock.

"Palm Valley looks like the setting for an improbable science-fiction movie. At any moment you feel that a papier-maché dinosaur will jerk creakily through these primitive trees. There is a pungent blue-flowered herb growing here, and the cliffs are smudged with the deceptively soft-looking fuzz of spinifex. Neatly arranged cypress pines stud the whole setting like cloves on a layer cake.

"The red of the gorge seems to be a living thing. The colour is as bright as fluorescent paint or an illuminated halloween pumpkin. It varies from finely-milled paprika to deep claret. It is a spectrum of every shade of red on earth, and it glows with a rich, primitive vitality."

We returned to Alice Springs late that afternoon—my head still burning—and flew out the next day: a hot, clear day, all gold and wine-red, like the background of a Raphael painting. Betty, still captivated by the colours of the Centre's landscape, continued her notes while I rested: "There it is again, the hot pink of the Centre, but 'pink' cannot convey the range of its subtle, vibrant, sometimes sullen tones. Persimmon, salmon, quince, coral, plum; you could only pin them down with a computerized spectrometer, click it over the landscape like a geiger counter to register each colour with mathematical accuracy."

The Centre inspires this sort of fantasy. While Betty jotted more notes I dozed fitfully. My fever had grown worse and I rested my head on the window as we flew high over the Macdonnells, heading south-west. I was gathering my strength for Ayers Rock.

The Desert's Rare Bounty

On the infrequent occasions when a rainstorm quenches Australia's drought-worn Centre, the sands respond with a seemingly miraculous transformation. Within days of the rainfall, plants burst through the soil and bloom, their brilliantly coloured flowers masking the brick-red earth. Round-leafed parakeelya smothers the ground in a purple blanket, green mulla mulla (opposite) jut like tiny minarets from rocky crevices, and even the seemingly dead branches of slender petalostylis erupt in yellow blooms.

The showiest of the Outback's wildflowers are the annuals. They soak up large quantities of water, which evaporate rapidly from their gaudy blossoms; but because they live only during wet periods they have no need to husband moisture. Before they wither, the annuals produce seeds that will give rise to the next flowering generation: drought-resistant seeds, such as those of Sturt's desert pea, which can lie dormant in the dry soil for more than ten years. In their coats are "growth inhibitors": water-soluble chemicals that prevent the seeds from reacting to minor showers. Only when the inhibitors are dissolved by enough rain to sustain the plant through its life-cycle do the seeds germinate.

Perennials, the other main group of flowering plants, tend to have less spectacular blooms: they live on through drought and cannot afford to use their supplies of food and water solely for the production of flowers. During the long droughts, species such as the slender petalostylis shed leaves to conserve moisture, and their stems may die; but their extensive root systems tap water deep in the soil, and they store food in their underground stem structures. When rain comes, the perennials are resurrected, sending up green shoots amid the dead ones.

The colours, perfumes and varied shapes of the Centre's wildflowers play a vital role in their fleeting existence; they attract insects and birds that help pollinate the flowers and scatter the seeds. Bees, for example, are particularly drawn to the purple blossoms of parakeelya; while birds such as honeyeaters flit from bloom to bloom, sipping nectar with their brush-tipped tongues. The bounty is soon over, however. A few weeks after a drenching rain the flowers wither and the desert resumes its parched appearance—until banks of rain clouds once more herald the Outback's colourful floral show.

A shaft of afternoon sunlight highlights a stand of green mulla mulla in its rocky setting. The fuzzy blossoms of this common Outback perennial, which have inspired its alternative popular name, "pussytail", are made up of a multitude of tightly packed flowerets growing on top of slender, two-foot-tall stalks.

Bushy clumps of one of the hundred or more mulla mulla subspecies burst forth in popcorn-like white blossoms after a heavy rain.

As the stems and golden flowers of a cluster of yellowtop begin to wither, the feathery seeds of the next generation appear.

Creeping vine-like over the sandy soil after a rainfall, Sturt's desert pea dangles blood-red flowers, each with a glossy black centre.

Resurgent after rain, a slender petalostylis grows a first delicate bloom and tiny new leaves.

The fragile stalks of a parakeelya spring up in exuberant growth amid the apparent infertility of the Centre's parched red sands.

Drawing upon hidden supplies of water, a field of round-leafed parakeelya transforms the desert with its harvest of purple blossoms.

5/ The Sacred Monoliths

One might liken Mount Conner to a walled, mediaeval city; or Mount Olga to a ruined temple or palace of a bygone Pharaoh. But there seems to be nothing to which Ayers Rock can be likened. CHARLES P. MOUNTFORD/ *BROWN MEN AND RED SAND*

In the beginning, according to Aboriginal myth, there was the Dreamtime —a period when the earth was flat and vacant, neither light nor dark, with all the substance of nature awaiting the coming of god-like heroes to give it form and life. And so it seemed to us, flying 200 miles southwest of Alice Springs through the haze of a bushfire that had washed the bright blue from the morning sky and swept the desert landmarks below into blank extinction. Such bushfires ignite regularly in the scorching Outback, burn fiercely and briefly, obliterating everything in the area, and then die out. Lost in smoke and haze, our little aeroplane droned through this Dreamtime world. Aboard, in addition to myself, were my wife Betty, my son Dominic, and Alison Edgecombe, our pilot.

Reality asserted itself again as we came out of the smoky haze and got our first good look at Ayers Rock from the air. It looked like a giant mollusc lying on the desert plain. We were not prepared for its chilling grandeur. Some people find Ayers Rock beautiful, but at that moment it seemed to me to personify a peculiarly masculine malevolence. I feared the Rock a little then, and I still do; it is dark and brooding, drenched in myth, stained by time and ancient blood.

We flew on, the Rock fading behind us in the haze; and then, about 20 miles west of it, I saw the Olgas. From a distance these mountains seemed to consist of a single, smooth, curved mass of rock; but when we got closer, the mass resolved itself into a cluster of giant domes separated from one another by narrow gorges and arranged in a semi-circle around a central valley. I liked the Olgas as instantly as I dreaded the Rock. For if the Rock had a harshly masculine quality, the rounded mountains of the Olgas seemed softly feminine, like fantasies in stone. When our aircraft banked slowly around the naked domes, I found it amazing that few people outside Australia had even heard of these geological marvels—amazing and pleasing, for there was no building, not so much as a tent, to mar their antiquity. And to add to my delight, between the Olgas and the Rock the desert was blooming; a sea of wildflowers rippled over the ridges of red sand and lapped at the bases of the domes.

We flew back, landed beside Ayers Rock and made our base there, eager to explore the lonely outcrops and the blooming desert around them, preserved now in the Ayers Rock-Mount Olga National Park. We were met at our camp by Ian Cawood, a Northern Territory Reserves Board ranger. He was to be our guide and had arranged to have a four-wheel-drive truck ready to help us explore larger areas than we could cover on foot. Ian proved to be a genial man, gifted with a rich knowledge of the natural history and Aboriginal mythology of his reserve. Perhaps this was why he always used the pungent Aboriginal names rather than the ugly European labels slapped on every natural feature of the Rock. And the monolith's sacred significance coloured every conversation I had with him under its sombre flanks during the hot, still days or beneath the glittering stars at night. Ian called the Rock *Uluru*, from the Aborigines' word for the fluted parallel grooves they cut in their wooden artefacts—grooves that resemble the gutters time has carved in the top of the Rock itself. How much more eloquent than Ayers Rock, the name given to it by the explorer W. C. Gosse in 1873, in honour of a premier of South Australia.

On that first day with Ian we spent hours walking around the Rock, as insignificant as a file of ants. I walked in a sick daze much of the time; the fever I had caught in the Simpson Desert smouldered in my head as I crunched along dry creek-beds and scrambled over fallen boulders, longing to slake my raging thirst at a cool, green pool. The Outback's Flying Doctor was not due to visit the Rock until later in the week, but meanwhile no patient had more to distract him from his own frailty.

The Rock, which Australians claim is the largest monolith in the world, is not a massive boulder dumped on the red sand plain, but the smooth top of a partially-buried sandstone mass whose visible part is five and a half miles in circumference and more than a mile wide at its broad western end. From east to west it is about two miles long, with walls that rise at an angle of some 80 degrees—too steep to climb in most places—to a height of 1,140 feet. Viewed close up, the Rock appears somewhat less malevolent than it seems from the air. It looks like a homogeneous mass, but in fact it is composed of layer upon layer of a gritty, feldspar-rich sandstone called arkose, which is veined by bands of conglomerate containing pebbles up to an inch in diameter. The arkose was deposited in the late pre-Cambrian Period in horizontal beds that were shifted by later upheavals into near-vertical layers. Now the ancient beds of arkose are most apparent on the Rock's summit, where deep, parallel gullies cut by rain-water run between the sandstone strata. Since soil cannot cling to the rounded back of the Rock, most plants have been unable to grow there; only a few native fig trees, tough acacias and clumps of spinifex have found footholds high above their normal habitat.

The coarse-grained sandstone of the Rock sinks at least 7,500 feet and perhaps as much as 20,000 feet below the plain, merging underground with a different type of conglomerate that forms the Olgas 20 miles away. Above ground the surface of the Rock is stained black where huge waterfalls have plunged from its top during thunderstorms. On these occasions the water pours down the parallel gullies with a terrifying roar, refreshing the thick stands of mulga that crowd round the Rock's base. Soon after each storm the Rock is bone dry again. But meanwhile a tiny fraction of the water finds its way through hairline cracks in the Rock's hard surface and rots the stone beneath, weakening the sub-surface layer until eventually layers of the hard crust slough off, a process that is aided by the wedging effect of frost. This type of weathering occurs fairly frequently on the Rock, and in such a way that the huge mass is gradually decreasing in size without appreciably altering in form. On some parts of the Rock, however, wind, water and stress-inducing fluctuations of temperature have gouged out numerous caves and pockets. (A more detailed account of the effects that the elements have on Outback landforms appears in the picture essay on pages 76-85.)

The Rock sits massively on the plain, surrounded by the debris that has peeled off and slipped down its flanks, burying small trees and bushes around its base and forming caves and crannies where owls, rock-wallabies and other marsupials live. Here the Pitjandjara tribe of Aborigines still paint their Dreamtime legends and hold sacred ceremonies. They have invested every feature of their sacred Uluru with significance. To them each cliff, boulder and cave is the work or the embodiment of some totemic being who appeared at the end of the Dreamtime. Thus a boulder near the north-eastern face is a Mala (Hare-Wallaby)

Sunlight enters a gully in the south face of Ayers Rock, casting a rocky reflection on the surface of Maggie Springs. The pool is filled by water that cascades from the top of the Rock after storms. The sheer walls shading Maggie Springs on three sides ensure that evaporation occurs slowly, making it one of the most reliable of Ayers Rock's 11 waterholes.

man, and another boulder beside it is a Mala woman; those rock-holes on the north-western face are the footprints of the fiendish dingo, Kulpunya, and that vertical slab of rock above them is Kulpunya himself.

Kulpunya features in Uluru's major legend, a tale that fascinated me because it integrates primitive man and wild nature so closely. He was created, so the story goes, by the Mulga-Seed tribesmen of the Petermann Ranges, to avenge an insult from the Hare-Wallaby people who lived at Ayers Rock. They laid out his skeletal frame—a mulga branch for a backbone, forked sticks for ears, the tail of a bandicoot, the teeth of a marsupial mole—and then the medicine men chanted songs to fill him with evil. The next morning their monster was growing: hair had sprouted, his teeth had grown larger and feet were appearing. They sang him into full creation until he was the size of a dog, with great teeth, and hair along his back and at the tip of his tail; then they turned him loose at the Rock. Lunba, the Kingfisher-woman, saw Kulpunya coming and gave the alarm, but many of the Hare-Wallaby people were asleep in the noonday heat, and he destroyed most of them. A tumble of boulders near the north face of the Rock represents the fleeing Hare-Wallaby women.

I scanned the northern cliff face for the vertical slab that the Aborigines believe was Kulpunya creeping up to attack the Hare-Wallaby people; but I saw only the mud nests of white-backed swallows, hidden under a spur of rock. Farther on I saw one of Lunba's descendants, a red-backed kingfisher, nesting in a hole in the bank of a dry pool. It disappeared when I startled it—a flash of blue, red and white. I pressed my ear to its nesting hole, listening to the whirr-chirrup of the chicks inside; it was similar to the noise my tape recorder makes when I rewind a cassette. In a shallow pool near by, some dead shield shrimps were floating; the inch-long, olive-green crustaceans looked like Jules Verne submarines, with button eyes on shield-shaped, protective carapaces and long-tailed, segmented bodies. The urgent flurry of their brief lives was over, but they had laid the eggs that would ensure the survival of the species. The desert winds might scatter the eggs, but they would not destroy them, because the eggs are so drought-resistant that they can remain fertile throughout the most arid conditions.

Life flourishes around the Rock because the rains that pour off its back collect in pools at its base. Even in an exceptionally dry season there is usually one permanent pool. The year of our visit there had been 36 inches of rain; there were sandpipers in the shadow of the Rock, and the park rangers had even spotted a great knot from Siberia—tundra-breeding waders that winter regularly in Australia, but never before seen so far inland. We walked beneath huge buttresses on the rugged western face, making for a waterhole that lies under the southern face. A nankeen kestrel soared outside a cave above us. Near by were nests of zebra finches, cupped in prickly acacia trees; we could hear the finches quarrelling by the pool as we approached. Unlike many other Australian finches, these birds make several trips a day to drink water: "Follow them if you're lost," Ian Cawood told us. "They usually don't stray more than a couple of miles from it."

I plucked some small black native plums from a bush and was savouring their tart aftertaste when I stumbled over an unseen branch, scaring a collared sparrowhawk from the brush ten yards ahead where it had been dismembering a zebra finch. By a tiny soak of water flickering with water scorpions hunting their prey, I knelt beside the dainty mauve flowers of a trigger plant, plucked a piece of grass and lightly stroked it across one of the flowers. At once, the flower's long, protruding central structure, which carries the flower's reproductive organs, swung over like a trigger to dust my mock insect with pollen. It was a convincing demonstration of just one of the mechanisms that enable such a delicate-looking plant to thrive in such a hard land.

Our waterhole lay ahead—a large, still pool set in a steep-sided gully cut in the wall of the Rock. White Australians call the pool Maggie Springs; the Aborigines call it Mutitjilda, and believe that it is filled not with water but with the blood of a totemic creature. It seemed a sacrilege to dip our hands into the pool and splash our hot faces. A few feet from the main pool was a tiny depression filled with no more than six inches of water. My son Dominic bent down and discovered that it was wriggling with life. Little green shoots of grass or reed, each about half an inch long, were jerking in the water; evidently larval caddis flies, still in their protective cases of plant matter, were moving about in the pool.

Ian Cawood told us that his Aboriginal friends come to mourn and weep by this tiny depression, which they regard as a home of their spirit dead. Nothing else could have better demonstrated the gulf between white and black cultures; the one so divorced from nature, the other so firmly rooted in it. But any momentary sense of reverence we felt disappeared abruptly as a flock of zebra finches buzzed overhead like children exploding from school. Near by, a small brown skink stirred sleepily on a warm, red stone.

Next morning Dominic and I explored some of the caves around the Rock; the wall of one cave was stained dark with blood cut from the

Stalactite-like sandstone formations crowd the roof of a cave in Ayers Rock. But unlike true stalactites, which form in limestone caverns from minerals deposited by slowly dripping water, these spurs came about as water wore away cavities in the rock. The same erosive forces produced the convoluted surface of the cave floor.

arms of warriors during secret rituals. But my examination of the caverns was cursory; I had decided that the best way to gauge the immensity of the monolith, after our walk around it, was to climb it. I had been told that on top of the Rock were water-filled holes that had contained tiny fish until a recent drought scorched them off. How the fish got to the Rock in the first place is a mystery, since the nearest river is more than a hundred miles away. Furthermore, on top of the Rock is Uluru Water, a pool in which the Aborigines believe a giant, multi-coloured mythical snake lies coiled in age-old sleep.

Stiff-legged and with hands groping upwards, Dominic and I started to clamber up the sloping flank of the Rock's north-west corner. In 1873 W. C. Gosse and his Afghan camel-driver, Kamran, climbed the much steeper southern face in bare feet. "How I envied Kamran his hard feet," the explorer wrote. "He seemed to enjoy the walking about with bare feet while mine were all in blisters, and it was as much as I could do to stand." Ours was a well-trodden climb, and Ian had "reassured" me that only four people had fallen to their deaths on the ascent. Still, it was a long haul and I cannot honestly say that I enjoyed it. A stiff breeze buffeted me when we reached the saddle of red rock and I had to fight against a recurring image of my body tumbling hundreds of feet through space to the plain beneath. After 20 minutes or so my throat burned so that I could scarcely breathe. I sat down just short of the summit while

Dominic disappeared over the final crest above me. "I could make it if my life depended on it," I told myself, "but it doesn't, so I won't." Honour thus restored, I enjoyed my eagle's-eye-view of the landscape.

The prospect from my vantage point was superb. To the west were the domes of the Olgas and a range of hills called the Sedimentaries. Surrounding these landmarks was the desert plain, dotted with dark-green mulga, lighter blotches of mallee scrub and clumps of spinifex. In places the plain was washed by the pastel tints of wildflowers. They would not live long in the desiccating Outback heat—long enough, however, to produce the seeds that would complete their life-cycle. Then the seeds would lie dormant, perhaps for years, until enough rain filtered down through the arid soil to leach away the chemical growth-inhibitors on their dry husks. When that happened, the seeds would sprout tender green shoots, flowers would bloom and the seeds of the next generation would be scattered to await the next rains. I gazed out over the plain until Dominic returned from the summit; then, slowly and nervously, I made my way down, ready now to explore the transitory garden that stretched away before us.

My first journey into the flowering desert was considerably less dramatic and less tinged with apprehension than my climb up the Rock. The wildflowers had been at their best some months before, in July and August, when there were frequent rainstorms; a botanist in Sydney had told me that by now I would see nothing. Happily she was wrong: the flowers may have passed their peak, but those still in bloom were far more beautiful than I had imagined. I had expected to see a wasteland; instead I found a virtual parkland, whose delicate and tenacious flowers had a spare and subtle charm that made the formal gardens of the Old World seem gaudy and overpainted. A sea of grey and green, lavender and pink masked the red earth that had been nourished by the recent, phenomenally heavy rains.

Of Australia's 15,000-odd plant species, only about 300 flourish in Ayers Rock-Mount Olga National Park; and these survive because of the various mechanisms they have evolved to help them withstand drought. Parakeelya, whose purple-pink flowers garlanded the sand, stores water in its thick, fleshy leaves and stem. Other species store moisture in underground tubers—a method so efficient that a tuber from one Australian desert plant displayed in the glass case of a New York museum produced a leafy shoot for six consecutive years before its water supply was exhausted. Most of the plants I saw growing around the Rock possessed tiny leaves, usually covered with a waxy skin or short hairs that reduce evaporation and shield the plant from excessive radiation. These coverings mask the green chlorophyll layers and account for the greyish-green hues that dominate Outback vegetation.

Early in the 1960s the plain between Ayers Rock and the Olgas was devastated by drought and denuded of many of its trees. But now, in the aftermath of several rainy years, it was studded by millions of young desert poplars—slender beauties more than 20 feet high. These trees were doomed to die at the onset of the next drought, attacked by insects and rabbits, felled by desert winds. Some skeletal victims of the last drought still stood, and on their branches sunbathing lizards were silhouetted against the blue dome of the sky. Near a withered trunk I saw an Australian bustard pacing solemnly through long golden grass, peering at us curiously. The bustard is a powerful flyer but uses its wings only as a last resort, even when threatened by danger. A man in a Land Rover once followed a bustard slowly for seven miles, waiting for it to fly. It never did, and the pursuer eventually gave up. Luckily, he was not hoping for the bird to lead him to water, because this bird, which lives on insects and seeds, has rarely been seen to drink.

In 1894 the Horn Scientific Expedition passed through this country. The expedition hoped to find oaks and beeches, elms and sycamores that had survived when the Centre dried up in the Pleistocene period, more than 10,000 years ago. The scientists were thousands of years too late to find deciduous forests, but their discovery of hitherto unknown desert plants and animals opened up new fields in the natural history of Australia. The expedition members found desolation, too, especially on the white salt surface of Lake Amadeus, 50 miles to the north of Ayers Rock; the only living thing they saw was a solitary, gaunt dingo that followed them silently until the sun sank. But the news they brought back from this desert was of a surprising richness of life, including 21 members of the daisy family and 14 grasses.

Now, we saw a similar wealth of life, including desert oaks, some of which stood more than 50 feet high, an incredible growth for the arid climate in which they lived. These oaks survive because their long, probing roots reach far underground to find moisture long after the surface has cracked from drought; and the oaks' cork-like bark is so thick that it insulates the sap-conducting layers in their trunks. Their leaves are mere needles that hang vertically to escape the full effect of the sun and minimize water evaporation in the hot winds. Here and there, young oaks resembled fuzzy feather dusters; they were ready to shed their leaves at the onset of the next drought and stand, apparently

A male Australian bustard peers above the grass of an Outback plain. Usually sleek and shy, the bird's appearance and behaviour change during courtship. Then, puffing up its feathers and arching its neck backwards to touch its raised and fan-like tail, it struts about in the open. As part of the courtship ritual it breaks its normal silence by emitting a booming call.

dead, waiting for a rainstorm to trigger their regrowth. To the Aborigines, the oaks represent an invading army of Liru—Poisonous Snake-people —who advanced on the Rock during the Dreamtime. The spears they hurled at the tribes beside the Rock were responsible, the Aborigines believe, for many of the holes that pock the sandstone mass.

The vegetation around Ayers Rock has served the Aborigines in diverse ways. They were tapping it for poisons and medicines long before botanists penetrated the Centre; and they had their own classification of plants, based on the uses they found for them. They extracted therapeutic oils from eucalyptus and they pulverized mulga seeds to make flour for their bread. We examined some *Duboisia hopwoodii* bushes, whose leaves yield a narcotic that the Aborigines call *pituri*. They used to chew the dried leaves, mix them with wood ash, and place them in pools or baited bowls to drug emus into easy capture.

We had barely started our walk through this desert garden when we spotted four emus: a male, with his distinctive white throat, protecting three of his young beneath a shady mulga tree. All fled before we could get near them, vanishing among witchetty bushes that shook as they raced through them. The witchetty bush, with its golden spikes and small black seeds, was also high on the Aborigines' larder-list. They ate the seeds and dug edible grubs that gathered around its long, straight roots; and they also used the roots to make spear-shafts. Farther on we

A tawny frogmouth at roost during the heat of the day adopts a rigid stance, relying on its mottled, bark-like colouring to escape detection by predators. After sunset, this sluggish nocturnal feeder swoops to earth and hunts for insects, small mammals and reptiles, which it scoops up in its broad, shovel-shaped beak.

found some paper-daisies, like those I had last seen in the Simpson Desert. Although they looked fresh, they were dead; their white flowers crumbled like ash between my fingers. In contrast, the fluffy, papery flowers of pink mulla mulla still flourished. A pale pink species, *Ptilotus obovatus*, formed mosaics with clumps of yellow spinifex six weeks after I had expected to find them withered. I was amazed at the sheer variety of the desert vegetation. In some places the tawny grasses and solitary, widely spaced trees reminded me of African lion country; in others the corkwood trees, profuse with big, orange-yellow bottle brushes, evoked the Orient.

An equally extraordinary variety of wildlife populate this varied habitat. Rock wallabies rest in the caves and crevices of Ayers Rock, while their large cousins, the red kangaroos, lie beneath mulga and desert oaks out on the plain. Five or six feet under the mulga scrub, in horizontal passages, live honey ants, their tiny heads mere appendages of bulging abdomens that are swollen with food stored against the next drought. In the spinifex clumps little grass-wrens flutter and skip after their insect prey. Tiny mice range over the whole area; when we startled them, they bounded along so swiftly that their long, thin legs disappeared in a blur and they looked like balls of down blown by the wind.

Over our heads flew a huge flock of budgerigars—so many that they blotted out a large patch of sky. The Outback budgerigars breed several times in a season when food is plentiful, sparking off massive population explosions, for the chicks are mature enough to breed within 60 days of leaving their nests. Mighty flocks then funnel out from the breeding grounds, bursting forth in brief coloured glory, stripping the seed from the land—until the next drought comes and the waterholes dry up. When that happens the budgerigars die and their green bodies lie heaped on the cracked, red mud. A cloud of surviving budgerigars spiralling down to a diminishing waterhole is a grim sight. Predators, like the little and brown falcons, are waiting, ready to snatch up stragglers. The birds drink in frantic haste, the first few hundred floating on the surface, wings spread and ready to fly off; others scoop a beakful in mid-flight. Latecomers are so desperate for water that they land on top of other birds, drowning them. At such times they will even alight on an outstretched hand cupping a few drops of the precious liquid. While the birds drink and thrash about in the pool, the crows wait patiently to claim the sodden bodies of those that have drowned.

Heat itself can be as remorseless a killer of the Centre's birds as lack of water. Ian Cawood discovered this as he was patrolling a valley in the

Sedimentaries, north-east of the Olgas one day, and came across a tawny frogmouth brooding two chicks. The mother-bird, disturbed from her daytime slumber, flew off when Ian was about 20 yards from the nest. He photographed the chicks and then hid in the scrub to await the mother's return. About ten minutes later he saw that the chicks were becoming agitated, opening their mouths wide in distress, so he promptly retreated to make sure that he was not scaring off the mother. An hour later he stole back to photograph the mother and chicks together, but she was still missing—and the chicks were dead. He took them out of the nest and was surprised to find how hot they were. "Lesson learnt," he reported to his superior. "Be careful not to disturb nocturnal animals during the heat of the day."

One of the most fascinating creatures we saw was the bird called the crimson chat. The chats are unique to Australia: nomadic desert birds that walk quickly—rather than hop—after insects. Sometimes they impale their insect prey on thorns before eating them. They have brush-like tongues that evidently enable them to extract nectar from desert flowers. The male's crimson crown, breast and rump make him one of the most brilliant of the Outback's birds. The family we found had built its cup-shaped nest of dry grass in the prickly top of a spinifex clump. A small, dead desert poplar protruded from the clump, partially hiding the nest and its chicks from predators, but it provided shade only during the first hour of daylight. When we discovered that the nest contained young, we settled down to watch the family.

The parent chats fed their brood swiftly, before the sunlight slanted on to the nest, the male doing most of the food gathering. He was away no more than five to eight minutes on each excursion, returning with little green grubs and caterpillars, plus the occasional small butterfly or moth. He made many more trips than did the female, but both observed a strict "await your turn" system of feeding the chicks. They hesitated sometimes, but invariably popped the food into the mouth of the right chick. The parents were rarely at the nest together; one bird usually waited near by until the other had finished feeding the young. Most fascinating of all was the chats' preoccupation with cleaning their nest—and the assistance that this species receives from nature. Cleaning was a ritual they observed on each visit. In fact, each parent seemed to wait to collect the droppings, which the chicks appeared to time for a moment when their parents were there. The droppings were encased in round, white sacs, which the parents picked up in their beaks and disposed of at some distance from the nest.

While we watched, a singing honeyeater landed on a branch close by. The female chat was absent; the male chat immediately began circling around on the ground, dragging one wing as if it were broken, an instinctive manoeuvre used to distract an intruder. The honeyeater, a non-predatory bird, took no notice, so the chat flew at it until it made off. One threat removed, a more serious one approached: the sun began to shine directly on the nest. The male chat flew on to the nest and straddled it—wings half-spread, beak wide open—breathing quickly. Through the heat of the day, the female returned with food, although less frequently, and the male sat alone shielding the chicks, his head and eyes constantly on the alert for danger.

We stayed in our camp near the Rock for several days, making many journeys into the plain in our four-wheel-drive truck. Each time we circled closer and closer to the Olgas, and at last, early one morning, we left our camp and set off towards the mysterious domes, travelling along a rough road that had been bulldozed through the Park in 1948. The road led through soft sand, sinking here and there in pools of water that splashed the truck with mud the colour and consistency of mustard. Along the way I heard the musical morse code of a shrike-thrush, and saw a mulga parrot explode from the scrub and flick out of sight, as if tugged by an invisible cord. But then my attention was drawn to the Olgas, whose violet-pink domes loomed like a fantasy above the ranks of desert poplars around their base. I felt that we should come bearing gifts, so strong was the impression of an ancient city. But no robed city fathers waited imperiously to greet us—only a wedge-tailed eagle that soared slowly up the spiralling thermals on its eight-foot wingspan.

Finally we stood in the foothills of the Olgas, and scrambled up a rocky slope towards their towering domes. Beneath an outcrop sat two euros, or hill kangaroos, looking like dark paper cut-outs in the shade of a gnarled mulga tree. Euros are stockier than Australia's more famous red kangaroos, and have pale muzzles, and black-tipped hair along their backs. These two specimens regarded us curiously for a moment, then bounded off into a gully, their broad, rough-soled hind feet firmly gripping the smooth rock and their little forelimbs held close to their bodies, like spinsters clutching their handbags. We were left alone beneath the silent domes.

We were at the eastern edge of the Olgas, whose 31 domes are compactly spread in a semi-circle over eight and a half square miles. The range takes its name from the largest dome, Mount Olga—named by the

19th-Century explorer Ernest Giles in honour of the Queen of Spain—which forms the western outpost of the group, and bulges nearly 1,800 feet above the plain. The domes are composed of a plum-pudding mixture of conglomerates: a hotch-potch of rounded pebbles, stones and boulders far more intriguing than the seemingly homogeneous arkose sandstone of Ayers Rock.

No one knows with certainty where this mixture came from or how it was transported to its present site. The most likely explanation is that it was torn from ranges far to the south-west by one of the many seas that inundated the interior of Australia in pre-Cambrian times. The fragments were rolled smooth as they were carried to the interior and there they were cemented in thick beds by deposits of fine sand. After the sea retreated, some upheaval in the earth's crust thrust these beds upwards, and in the 500 million to 600 million years since then they have weathered into the present domes. Today they can be seen clearly from a distance of 50 miles when the desert air is clear.

Steep, narrow valleys between the domes mark where the forces of erosion have carved through zones of weakness in the ancient beds. But their walls are amazingly smooth; the boulders and the siliceous cement between them have worn away at the same rate. The sun shines only briefly into the chasms and clefts, and here we found rock-pools surrounded by vines and other moisture-loving plants. These gorges also provide a haven for animals: mammals, lizards, snakes, spiders and birds occupy the protective shade.

We walked down a large chasm, passing white ghost gums that clustered along a creek-bed within the gorge. Lemon-flowered gums grew on the slopes above us; the yellow blooms of cassia shone in the gloom. We heard the noisy squabbling of zebra finches nesting in low acacia bushes along the base of the chasm. At the other end of the gorge we emerged into a vast, grassy valley so park-like that I half expected to see iron railings, courting couples and children flying kites.

Tiny yellow seed-cups were strewn like shells on the earth. A cool breeze blew down the valley, bringing the faint smell of bushfire smoke. This wind blows constantly through the Olgas (the central valley is called the Valley of the Winds); it was thought by the Aborigines to be the breath of a sacred serpent that lived in a great cavern inside Mount Olga. If anyone infringed strict tribal law, this serpent's breath would become a vengeful hurricane. Today, the elders claim, the serpent lies coiled in eternal sleep and can no longer keep the people from transgressing the laws of the tribe.

The Olgas drew us back again and again. In our truck we circled them on a road too bone-shaking for ordinary vehicles; and we explored them on foot. We filed into the Valley of the Mice Women, on the southern side of the group, where a tiny stream sparkled beneath the dome of the Dying Kangaroo Man. The smooth, red rock above us was streaked as if by black brush-marks, where water had cascaded after each rain, leaching minerals from the stone. The valley was still and sunny, strewn with stone chips the Aborigines had left. We lingered in the valley until after sunset, wondering at the glitter of stars through tangled branches and watching out for the owls perched on trees and in rock crevices. They were listening for any sound that might betray their prey, before swooping down on soft, silent wings.

Climbing around the Olgas, we gazed over the desert at the distant Musgrave Ranges to the south, north towards the forbidding salt wastes of Lake Amadeus, and always upwards at the great domes, unclimbable without knowledge of the hidden routes. I rested one afternoon by a string of rock-pools in Walpa Gorge, beneath Mount Olga. Here mythical Corkwood Tree-women were said to have soaked tree blossoms in the pools to make a sweet drink; near by, the Poisonous Snake tribes camped on their way to attack Ayers Rock. Peace fills the Olgas now, a timeless peace that moved the explorer Ernest Giles to write: "There they have stood, as huge memorials of the ancient times of earth, for ages—countless aeons since its creation first had birth. Time, the old, the dim magician, has ineffectually laboured here, although with all the powers of ocean at his command; Mount Olga has remained as it was born."

Amid the silent domes I became aware how shallow and ephemeral were most of the issues of daily life I had temporarily left behind: the petty preoccupation with bills, learning to drive a car, contracting a mortgage or arranging a loan. None of them was of lasting worth.

At last, the Flying Doctor arrived at Ayers Rock and prescribed antibiotics for me; they should arrive, he said, on the next aircraft from Alice Springs. They never did arrive, but it did not matter; the Olgas had cured my fever.

NATURE WALK / To the Valley of the Winds

The sun was rising in the Ayers Rock –Mount Olga National Park. It threw long shadows as I tramped towards the distant Olgas, whose mauve domes were wreathed in a haze of bushfire smoke. Behind me, persimmon-red sand ridges, splashed here and there with green and yellow vegetation, rippled gently towards Ayers Rock. The tawny earth and the tree-studded plain evoked memories of the African veld; but the resemblance was superficial. This wildlife reserve never echoes to the thunder of galloping herds; its creatures are less majestic and far less obtrusive than those that roam the African plains. Most are nocturnal, rarely venturing out during the day from their lairs in bush, burrow or cave. To observe them you need time and a great deal of patience.

Patience was something I had learned to acquire during my Outback journey, and I had plenty of time, for it would be several hours before I reached my destination: a summit overlooking the Valley of the Winds, which lies within the heart of the Olgas. A stream, Bubia Creek which had filled after recent rain, has its source near that summit. Water is so scarce in Australia's Centre that it acts as a magnet for wildlife. I knew that if I followed Bubia Creek to its source beneath the domed hump of Mount Ghee, one of the western outposts of the Olgas, I stood a good chance of seeing many of the more elusive Outback creatures.

Tracks in the Sand

I jammed on my old slouch hat, checked to make sure my water-bottle was full, and set off towards the beckoning domes. As I walked, my boots rasped on sand that was embroidered with the tiny tracks of small mammals and shy desert birds. The sun was now well above the horizon, and most nocturnal animals would have retired to their cool, dark lairs; but I took care to tread softly up each sand ridge in the hope of surprising some straggler caught in the open by the rising sun.

My route lay at first through a maze of spinifex clumps and I was glad I wore long socks with my shorts: from a distance, the five-foot-wide tussocks looked silken-soft, but when I brushed against them their brittle, yellow leaves stabbed me with their needle-sharp tips. Dead grey mulga branches, the relics of past droughts, were strewn like old bones between the spinifex clumps. Scattered among them were

SPINIFEX AGAINST THE DISTANT SILHOUETTE OF THE OLGAS

reminders of brief flowerings to come: shiny black seeds so hard that they crackled when I tried to snap them between my fingers.

Farther on, rich green trees and bushes rose from among the spinifex, and the red sand was masked in places by a multicoloured wash of wildflowers. I passed the tall, erect

DESERT GREVILLEA

stems of desert grevillea, a shrub whose flowers are such a striking orange they seem to capture the essence of the sun. The shrubs stood up to ten feet tall, their inch-long flowers growing in cone-like clusters on the ends of their stems. The blooms are so rich in nectar that nomadic Aborigines, striding through this wilderness, used to bend the stems down, pluck the flowers and suck them like lollipops to sweeten their mouths during long desert journeys. Now, few Aborigines pass this way: the flowers of desert grevillea are left for nectar-eating birds such as the brown honeyeater, whose plaintive, five-noted song I heard close by.

Nearer the Olgas, a cool breeze stirred the leaves of young desert poplars and desert oaks. I paused

MILITARY DRAGON

on the crest of a ridge to rest in the shade of a spiky, green acacia tree, one of a group of Outback trees called dead finish because they grow in such dense thickets that are virtually impenetrable.

A splash of colour on the sunny incline of the ridge caught my eye; looking around, I saw the yellow-striped body of a lizard about four inches long. It was a military dragon, tiny cousin of the fierce-looking bearded dragon, and it was basking in the full glare of the sun in order to raise its blood temperature and stimulate its circulation. To speed up the warming process (a necessary part of the daily cycle of reptiles, which cannot generate their own body heat), the lizard had raised itself on its forelimbs and spread-eagled its hind limbs, thus increasing the heat-absorbing surface area of its body. Later, as the day grew hotter, the lizard would protect its body from overheating by moving to the shady side of the ridge or retreating to some cool crevice.

A column of small, black ants was marching towards the military dragon, but the lizard was still too cold and sluggish to show any interest in this potential meal. Only when I disturbed it did it move, skittering into a hole among the tangled roots of a clump of spinifex. The ants had gained a stay of execution.

As I walked on towards the Olgas, I marvelled at the wealth of plant life on this desert plain. There were literally millions of desert poplars, and among them stands of mulga and bloodwood trees. In fact, amid all this vegetation I almost overlooked one of the most fascinating of all Outback plants: the kerosene grass, which grew in pale green and yellow clumps around my feet.

Self-Burying Fruits

When I realized what the plant was, I stopped to perform an Outback trick. From one clump I removed a tiny, three-branched, stem-like fruit, moistened its base in my mouth, then stuck it into the ground. Immediately it began twisting round like a helicopter's rotor blades, screwing itself into the sand to a depth of nearly an inch. In case the breeze might be propelling it, I repeated the manoeuvre with another

FRUIT OF KEROSENE GRASS

"stem"—this time in the lee of a ridge where not a leaf stirred. Again it buried itself.

The secret of the grass is revealed in its structure. The quarter-inch-long, conical germinating fruit is enclosed in a hard, scaly coat. From its top project three strands, wrapped tightly round one another in a spiral column. When the base becomes moist the strands untwist, causing the fruit below to rotate slowly, drilling into the sand. In this remarkable way the fruit plants itself after rain.

While I was studying the kerosene grass, I realized with a start that I was sitting beside a nest of the bulldog ant, a formidable member of the world's most primitive ant genus, the *Myrmecia*. A male, probably a soldier, guarded the entrance to the nest. I did not provoke him, for I

RATTLEPOD

knew that he was capable of inflicting a painful bite with his powerful, toothed mandibles, as well as administering an agonizing sting. Nor had I any intention of delving into the nest to find a female; she is bigger than the male—up to an inch long—and has weapons to match her greater size.

Bulldog ants are fiercely territorial, as many campers find when they pitch tents too near a nest. One old Outback hand, a prospector named Jim Escreet, combats the ant menace in a novel way. Quoted in *The Red Centre* by Keith Willey, he says: "I bring some ants from one nest and put them on another, along with a piece of tucker (food). By and by they get to fighting. Well, I get a couple of day's peace during the battle, another couple while they're burying their dead and a couple more while they celebrate."

Not far from the ants' nest, I came across some pools of water, left from a recent rain and lying like molten lava on the orange mud. Around their fringes, wildflowers garlanded the moist sand. I recognized the blazing yellow petals of rattlepod and the erect green crowns of mulla

BULLDOG ANT AT ENTRANCE OF NEST

GREEN MULLA MULLA

ROUNDED RAMPARTS OF THE OLGAS

A PERENTY

mulla, shaped like British guardsmen's bearskin helmets.

Resisting the temptation to linger and identify more beautiful blossoms, I continued my hike. I was close to the Olgas now; their smooth, red summits formed sinuous curves high above the green plain. I walked parallel to them for a distance, amid clumps of acacias. I flushed several emus that fled with heavy grace, and a red kangaroo that hopped ten yards then froze to watch me. About a mile out from the domes I came face to face with a dragon—well, a dragon of sorts. It was a perenty, Australia's largest lizard, which can grow to more than six feet in length. This specimen was

A CHEQUERED SWALLOWTAIL

only half that size, but nevertheless it was a splendid creature, with jewel-like eyes and pale yellow rosettes marking its throat. It was half asleep in the sun, and merely flicked its red tongue as it idly contemplated me. I realized why it was so drowsy when I saw a half-eaten rabbit beside it. Perenties can run at 20 miles an hour over short distances in pursuit of prey, but this specimen was digesting its meal and was reluctant to exert itself. It ambled off at last, splay-legged, waddling along, for all the world like a baby in a wet nappy.

I did not wait to see where the lizard went: I was anxious to reach the flanks of the Olgas, where I knew I could find cool, fresh water and shade. I headed towards Bubia Creek, which flows down from a narrow gorge alongside Mount Ghee, threading my way through feathery kangaroo grass. A wedge-tailed eagle was soaring above the domes, and a brown falcon flapped low over a screen of trees ahead, pestered by two impudent willie-wagtails. Beyond the trees was the creek, a pure, sparkling stream that gurgled between the rock-strewn slopes. A butterfly was drinking on the moist earth of the bank; it was a chequered swallowtail, a strong flyer common in the Centre.

I drank sparingly, filled my water-bottle, then followed the creek towards Bubia Gorge. All around me rose the immense rock domes: many were cracked in places, as if bolts of lightning had struck them; others were streaked black where run-off water had leached manganese oxide from the rock. Farther upstream, I found fresh dingo tracks at the water's edge. A few feet away, a tangle of native oats glistened in the water; looking closer, I noticed the cast-off skins of dragonfly larvae, and a newly emerged specimen—an imago—clinging to the grassy stalks.

I decided to explore the steep dome sides before continuing along the creek, and so I clambered up a rock-strewn slope on my right. Rock clinked on rock as I climbed, and occasionally I skirted fallen red boulders that lay broken open, revealing a nougat-like mixture of earth and smooth stones. Between the shards of stone, the earth was ablaze with yellow billy buttons and the fluffy flowers of pink mulla mulla. These wildflowers were bright

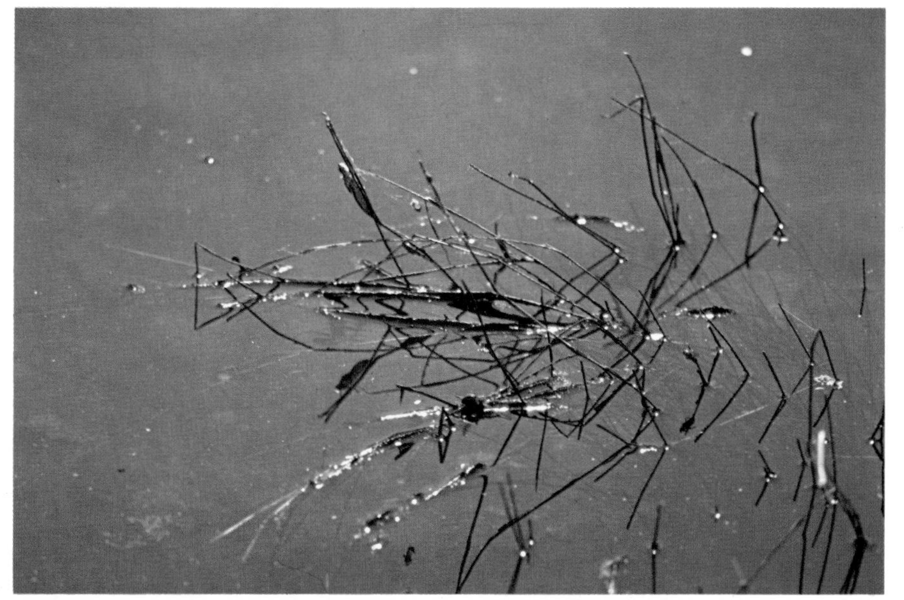

IMAGO OF A DRAGONFLY ON NATIVE OATS

FOOTHILLS OF THE OLGAS VIEWED FROM A CAVE

daubs of colour amid the glossy green leaves of native hops and bloodwood trees, many of whose branches were festooned with the red flowers and smooth, flat leaves of mistletoe.

I headed up towards a series of caves scalloped in the base of the dome. Aborigines once lived in these caves; their carvings and paintings adorn many of them. But now the sole inhabitants are the creatures of the Outback. I hauled myself up into the first cavern, some 300 feet above the plain. Euros, or hill kangaroos, rest here during the heat of the day, gazing down on the silent green foothills into which they descend at evening to feed. Perhaps they had seen me coming, for the cave was now empty, and only the fresh droppings on the floor betrayed their recent presence.

I clambered along the slope and glanced into a second cave; another euro retreat. Its walls were streaked with bat droppings and its roof was plastered with crumbling, abandoned mud-wasp nests. A nankeen kestrel fluttered out of a dark hole farther along the cliff face; but nothing else stirred, and the only thing that broke the silence was an unseen bird singing far below.

I sat at the mouth of the cavern for some time, gazing ahead along the cave-dotted ramparts of Bubia Gorge. After a quick snack of dried fruit and a gulp of water, I scrambled back down the slope to resume my exploration of the creek.

A Euro Trail

I was examining some holes scratched in the bank of the stream by an echidna, or spiny anteater, in its search for food, when I spotted a trail curving up through dense, spiky bushes in a steep-sided, narrow valley between two domes. I guessed that it had been made by euros coming down from their rocky retreats to drink. I had seen euros on my first trip to the Olgas, but I wanted a closer look at these kangaroos so I decided to follow the trail in the faint hope of finally tracking down one. The steady breeze that wafts around the domes of the Olgas was welcome as I fought my way up the foot-wide

CAVE ENTRANCE IN THE OLGAS

track, pushing aside branches that scratched my face and snagged my clothing. The trail curved up through a mass of broken rock and eventually I came to a jumble of boulders beneath one of the domes. Beyond the boulders was a cavern about 50 feet high—much higher than the other caves—and from it issued the humming of thousands of blowflies.

I climbed the boulders and entered the cave, which had been formed when a slab of rock slipped down to the base of the dome. It had come to rest at an angle, and between it and the dome there was a huge triangular space. The underside of the slab was studded with big, round stones that looked as if they had been pressed into the conglomerate by some giant hand, like raisins into pastry. Apart from the flies, I found the cavern empty; but outside, a dark grey western shrike-thrush warbled in a near-by thicket, and two grey-headed honeyeaters hopped on to a spearbush at the entrance of the cavern and peered inquisitively in at me.

STURT'S DESERT ROSE

Disappointed that I had failed to spot a euro, I struggled back down the trail, adding to my scratches and wishing that euros were taller and more broad-shouldered. Back at the creek, I saw shrubs of Sturt's desert rose, a pink hibiscus-like flower with a raspberry red centre, which is the floral emblem of the Northern Territory. Near by was a small pool, and as I approached it I heard the buzzing of wasps. They were gathering mud and mixing it with saliva to make their nest-building material. Rolling it into balls where the water met the sand, they flew off with it towards the caves I had left, to build their mud cylinders, which they would stock with caterpillars for their offsprings' food supply.

As soon as they had left, a flock of zebra finches fluttered down to the pool, perched on fallen branches that protruded from the water, and leaned down to drink. They did not raise their heads so that the water would run down their throats, as most birds do, but sucked it up as if through a straw. They drank quickly to minimize the time they were exposed to danger, then they departed

MUD WASPS COLLECTING NEST-BUILDING MATERIAL

ZEBRA FINCHES DRINKING

BUDGERIGARS DECORATING A DEAD OAK

in a nervous flurry. They left the pool open in turn to a group of budgerigars, which until then had perched near by, decorating the branches of a dead desert oak like colourful buds. The budgerigars swooped down, scooping up beakfuls of water before themselves departing in a flurry of green and yellow.

Music in the Desert

A poet once damned Australia as a songless land. He must have been deaf; for all day as I walked and climbed I heard the song of birds. High above me rufous songlarks trilled their rich, melodious whistle; while deep in the thickets I heard the piping calls of western shrike-thrushes. Now I heard a bird-song that eclipsed those others and, following the sound, I saw a pied butcher-bird perched on a bough as it sang. Suddenly I understood the haste of the zebra finches a few minutes before. The butcher-bird is a predatory species with a sharp hook at the tip of its long upper mandible; it is a fierce pursuer of small birds and reptiles. Like the unrelated shrikes of Europe and America (which often are also called "butcher-birds"), it spikes its victims on the ends of twigs, or wedges them in clefts between branches before tearing them to pieces and eating them. But unlike the shrikes it does not make "larders"—stores of surplus food. And there is another important difference: the butcher-birds of other countries have a grating call, but this specimen was stretching its black throat in a beautiful flute-like song that stopped me dead. Here in the heart of the wilderness, it was delivering the opening bars of Beethoven's Fifth Symphony. The liquid notes spilled out as on and on it sang. Another joined it in a duet and both birds sang in unison, dipping their heads as if in mutual acknowledgement of their artistry.

The birds were still singing as I left, the sound carrying up the gorge. Farther upstream, the creek cascaded into a string of rock pools. I lay down beside one and drank deeply of the clear water—perhaps the most delicious drink I have ever had. It was certainly in the most

A PIED BUTCHER-BIRD IN SONG

spectacular setting: the silent domes of the Olgas were mirrored in the calm water, and pale blue and red dragonflies sailed low over the surface, their whirring wings sounding like elastic bands being strummed. I saw one of them resting, strangely still, on a plant with delicate white flowers that glistened in the sunlight at the edge of one of the pools. I walked over to investigate and saw that the dragonfly was dead: a victim of the insectivorous Indian

INDIAN SUNDEW—AND VICTIM

sundew plant. The dragonfly is itself a predator, so it could not have been attracted to the sugary glue that the plant exudes to trap its insect victims. It probably had alighted on the plant to rest, and had been caught by the hairy, glandular, sticky tentacles on the leaves and stem of the sundew. Struggling to free itself, the dragonfly had become more firmly trapped, each tentacle transmitting a stimulus to the others so that they all curled over to enfold their prey. Now the tentacles were secreting a digestive juice from the glands at their tips to absorb the nutrients from the insect. In a matter of days the iridescent blue body of the dragonfly would disintegrate. Then the sundew's tentacles would straighten out, and the plant would wait, innocently beautiful, for its next victim to come along.

About 50 yards farther on, the creek splashed down a steep slab of rock, forming a pool where I bathed my feet. Beside the pool I saw what at first appeared to be a small twig lying among the pebbles. Then I noticed that the twig was moving: it was a stick insect, a common tree-living species, crawling slowly across the earth in its laborious journey from one plant to another to feed. This specimen was missing a leg—no doubt the result of a close escape from a predatory bird. Although it was not entirely safe while in the open like this, its camouflage colouring and unusual shape provided partial protection.

Clumps of rock isotome, a perennial herb with pale blue flowers, grew at the side of the waterfall. The prettiness of the plant effectively disguises its poisonous nature—the Aborigines used to extract a milky sap from its succulent stems to use as a narcotic; the sap can also cause a temporary, but agonizing, blindness if rubbed into the eyes.

I was almost at the source of the creek now, my long walk to view the Valley of the Winds nearly over. On my left, high above me, was a narrow gorge cut between the steep walls of two domes. I left the stream and climbed up towards the gorge, hoping to get a panoramic view of the valley from its crest. In a thicket by the mouth of the gaping cleft, I suddenly came upon an agitated willie-wagtail sitting on a nest in a small tree and swinging its tail from side to side in alarm as I approached. It fluttered off the nest and perched on a tree as I came closer, uttering

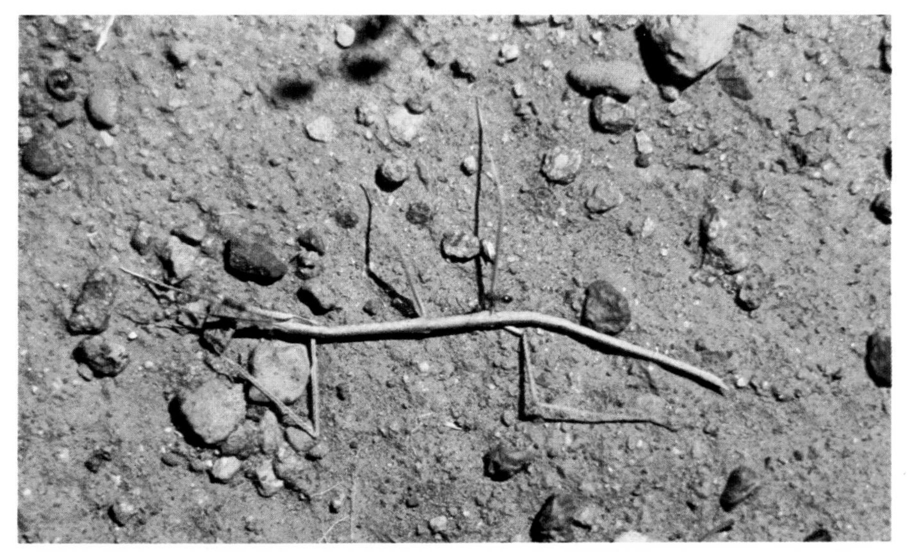

A WELL-CAMOUFLAGED STICK INSECT

WILLIE-WAGTAIL GUARDING NEST

harsh, clattering notes—completely unlike its familiar song, which sounds like "sweet-pretty-creature". It hopped from branch to branch with great agitation when I inspected the nest, a cup of dried grass interwoven with strands from cobwebs. Inside was a greyish egg spotted with brown and a tiny chick only a few hours old. I moved away quickly when I saw the wagtail had young, looking back to make sure the bird returned to the nest.

Into Bubia Gorge

I was climbing steeply now, into the head of Bubia Gorge. The rock walls on either side rose almost vertically, threatening, it seemed, to topple over and engulf me. This gorge had been cut, over millions of years, by the action of water flowing over a layer of softer rock—now eaten away—between two domes.

The longest and most difficult part of my walk was now behind me. I reached a sheltered area nestling high in the Olgas, where a green rim of foliage grows. I began the final, short ascent, surrounded by daisies and mint bushes. I climbed to the edge of a ridge beneath the summit of Mount Ghee, stood beside a desert fig tree and looked out at the Valley of the Winds, surrounded by *Katatjuta*—the Many Heads—as the Aborigines call the majestic Olgas. The domes were so round and smooth, they looked as if they had been packed down and carefully shaped by some enormous jelly-mould.

With the afternoon sunshine slanting from the west, the domes cast broad shadows that crept slowly across the valley below me. I saw the dark green clumps of acacias amid the yellow spinifex on the plain—tiny "oases" in the centre of the desert. Even in the light of day I had a sense of the spirits with which the Aborigines peopled the Olgas; the empty stillness seemed ripe for some unearthly visitation.

The only thing that broke the silence was the sharp, whistling call of a wedge-tailed eagle, soaring in the blue sky far above me. I followed its graceful flight until it landed in a hole pitted high in the sheer wall of one of the domes. Over centuries the climate had fashioned this rocky eyrie from which the eagle could survey its killing-ground.

Before starting back in the now cooling afternoon, I spotted some figs on a tree beside me. The tree's twisted roots clung to the bare rock of the ridge, yet in this seemingly inhospitable setting its branches grew luxuriant leaves and ripe red and yellow fruit. I plucked one and savoured its bitter tang, while a soft breeze rustled through the leaves and streamed into the valley below.

THE VALLEY OF THE WINDS, PROTECTED BY THE ENCIRCLING OLGAS

6/ Explorers of the Ghastly Blank

Let any man lay the map of Australia before him, and regard the blank upon its surface, and then let me ask him if it would not be an honourable achievement to be the first to set foot in its centre. CHARLES STURT/ *AN ADDRESS TO THE COLONISTS OF ADELAIDE*

As I looked down on the Outback wilderness from the comfort of the aeroplane, I often wondered about the explorers who had braved those inhospitable wastes on the backs of camels or horses—and on foot. Their names, with few exceptions, have not been written large in the history books, as those of men like Stanley, Scott and Speke have been. Their exploits, although often graphically recorded, have not caught the public imagination to the same extent as other, sometimes lesser feats in other parts of the globe. The reason for their obscurity probably lies in the nature of the country they risked their lives to explore; Australia lacks the dramatic elements that so excited early travellers in other continents. No Himalayas rise from its inland plain; no Amazon flows down from its highlands; no lost civilizations lie hidden in its heart. The explorers founded no great cities. Their names persist only because of the plants and animals they found, or because they are attached to locations on the map. And the mountains, rivers and deserts that so often swallowed the hopes—and lives—of the explorers remain as wild today as when they were first crossed.

The explorer who intrigues me most is Ernest Giles, the man who named the Olgas, and whose tracks I crossed many times during my own travels in the Centre. Although by no means the most celebrated of the inland explorers, Giles is the one I most respect because he was an explorer simply for the love of it. He was also an incurable romantic and a kind of poet who genuinely marvelled at the wilderness that so often nearly destroyed him. "The pleasure and delight of visiting new and totally unknown places are only whetted by his [an explorer's] first attempt," he wrote. "The romance is in the achievement of difficult and dangerous, if not almost impossible, tasks. An explorer is an explorer from love, and it is nature, not art, that makes him so."

Few men were better qualified to speak of "almost impossible tasks". Giles once staggered 60 miles through a desert with a 50-pound keg of water on his back, knowing that to abandon it was death. This incident took place in 1873, when Giles and the other members of his expedition were attempting to make a first crossing of the Centre on horseback from Oodnadatta, on the southern fringe of the Simpson Desert, to the west coast. They were continually attacked by Aborigines, and, being short of food and water, halted and pitched camp near a dry creek in the Rawlinson Ranges, about 300 miles west of Ayers Rock. Giles and another man, Alfred Gibson, set out westwards by horse to search for more water, but after 90 miles one of their two mounts died of dehydration. Giles, unselfishly thinking to give Gibson the better chance of survival, sent him for help on the remaining horse and started to follow on foot. Weak with hunger and thirst, he tramped 30 miles to a water keg he and Gibson had left behind for just such an emergency and, when there was still no sign of Gibson, he picked it up and carried on, bending almost double under its weight. For seven days he supplemented his diet as only a starving man could. "I heard a faint squeak, and looking about I saw . . . a small dying wallaby, whose marsupial mother had evidently thrown it from her pouch. . . . The instant I saw it, like an eagle I pounced upon it and ate it, living, raw, dying—fur, skin, bones, skull and all. The delicious taste of that creature I shall never forget." By such expedients Giles managed to reach camp, but Gibson was never seen again; the desert that claimed his life bears his name.

Giles suffered other hardships. On his first expedition in 1872, an attempt to "push across the continent . . . to the settled districts of Western Australia", he floundered with his horses into Lake Amadeus, 50 miles north of the Olgas, sinking up to his thighs in hot salt mud. The horses were nearly lost: "It seemed an eternity," he recorded later. "They staggered at last out of the quagmire, heads, backs, saddles, everything covered with blue mud, their mouths were filled with salt mud also." On Giles's third expedition in 1875, a 1,400-mile trek on camels from Beltana, in South Australia, to Perth, he took the desperate gamble of finding water in the vast desert that blocked his party's path.

Pushing through spiky clumps of spinifex that opened festering wounds on their legs, they travelled for 16 days without finding an oasis. Some 325 miles into the wasteland, that Giles named the Great Victoria Desert, having "penetrated into a region utterly unknown to man, and as utterly forsaken by God", the expedition at last stumbled across a little spring, which Giles also dedicated to Queen Victoria. Later he discovered that, if they had missed the oasis, they would have had to press on another 200 miles before encountering water.

In spite of enduring all these hardships, Giles never lost the gentle self-mockery that was so much part of his character, and when despair rose all around him he still managed to joke wryly with his companions. He recorded a conversation with Saleh, his Afghan camel driver, when they were camped one night in the desert. "Mister Gile, when you get water?" Saleh asked. Giles pretended to laugh. "Water? Pooh! There's no water in this country, Saleh. I didn't come here to find water; I came here to die, and you said you'd come and die too." Saleh pondered this for a while before continuing: "I think some camel he die tomorrow, Mr. Gile." "No, Saleh, they can't possibly live till tomorrow. I think they will all die tonight." Saleh: "Oh, Mr. Gile, I think we all die soon now." Giles: "Oh yes, Saleh, we'll all be dead in a day or two."

"When he found he couldn't get any satisafaction out of me he would begin to pray," Giles wrote. "He would ask me which way was the east. I would point south; down he would go on his knees and abase himself in the sand, keeping his head in it for some time. Afterwards he would have a smoke, and I would ask: 'What's the matter Saleh? What have you been doing?' 'Ah, Mr. Gile,' was his answer, 'I been pray to my God to give you a rock-hole tomorrow.' I said: 'Why Saleh, if the rock-hole isn't there already, there won't be time for your God to make it; besides, if you can get what you want by praying for it, let me have a fresh-water lake, or a running river. . . . What's the use of a paltry rock-hole?' Then he would say solemnly: 'Ah, Mr. Gile, you not religious.' "

Sadly, Giles's expeditions into the Centre—five in all—achieved little in terms of opening up overland routes, and his exploits fade when compared with those of the other inland explorers. The sagas of Charles Sturt, the mysterious fate of Ludwig Leichhardt, the miserable end of Burke and Wills—these are the adventures that do more to capture the imagination. When Giles died in 1897, he was working as a £3-a-week office clerk in Coolgardie, Western Australia, more or less forgotten.

If Giles never received recognition, perhaps it did not worry him too much; he was not, after all, in pursuit of glory. What kept him going on

Striding ahead of his caravan in 1875, Ernest Giles leads his third expedition on its 1,400-mile journey from Beltana to Perth.

his desert journeys, he said, was a burning desire to "tread where no white man's foot had ever wandered". But what motivated the other Outback explorers to attempt again and again the same terrible desert crossings? What made them risk pain, thirst, hunger, heat, cold, exhaustion, disease and danger in the barren uncharted wilderness?

Some of the explorers were fortune-seekers, particularly after 1851 when gold was discovered in New South Wales. Before that date there were rewards for those who could find new pasture-lands for the developing colonies and blaze overland trails to improve communications and the movement of stock. For others, the great white space on the map of Australia—the Ghastly Blank as it came to be called—offered a challenge to any adventurer in search of a reputation. Some explorers, like Edward Eyre, used their record as a springboard to high positions in the British Empire; and John Forrest, a native-born Australian who made some of the fastest and most useful inland crossings of the 1870s, saw his pioneering journeys as no more than his solemn duty to the new nation. There were others like him, but I suspect that in every one of them there was something of Giles: the curiosity, the desire to see over the next ridge and even, indeed, beyond the horizon.

The distant horizon must have been a tantalizing prospect, for many of the early explorers believed that somewhere in the interior of Australia there existed a huge, freshwater inland sea. In the 1820s, a few years after a path into the interior had been hacked across the Blue Mountains of the Dividing Range west of Sydney, one of the great puzzles was what happened to the rivers that flowed inland from the watershed of the Dividing Range. Their outlets had not been discovered on the continent's coasts and expeditions down the Lachlan and Macquarie rivers, which flow across the south-eastern corner of Australia, had been halted by seemingly impassable marshes. Surely beyond those marshes there was an inland sea into which the rivers drained?

In 1829, the Governor of New South Wales, Sir Ralph Darling, decided that the puzzle of the rivers must be solved. The most likely route to the inland sea was thought to be the Murrumbidgee, a wide, fast-flowing river draining from the ranges behind Mount Dromedary, near the present site of Canberra. The governor ordered his young military secretary, Captain Charles Sturt, of the 39th Foot, to mount an expedition to trace the Murrumbidgee to its outlet. Sturt was no stranger to exploration; the previous year he had mapped much of the area around the Macquarie and discovered Australia's longest river, which he had named the Darling after his sponsor.

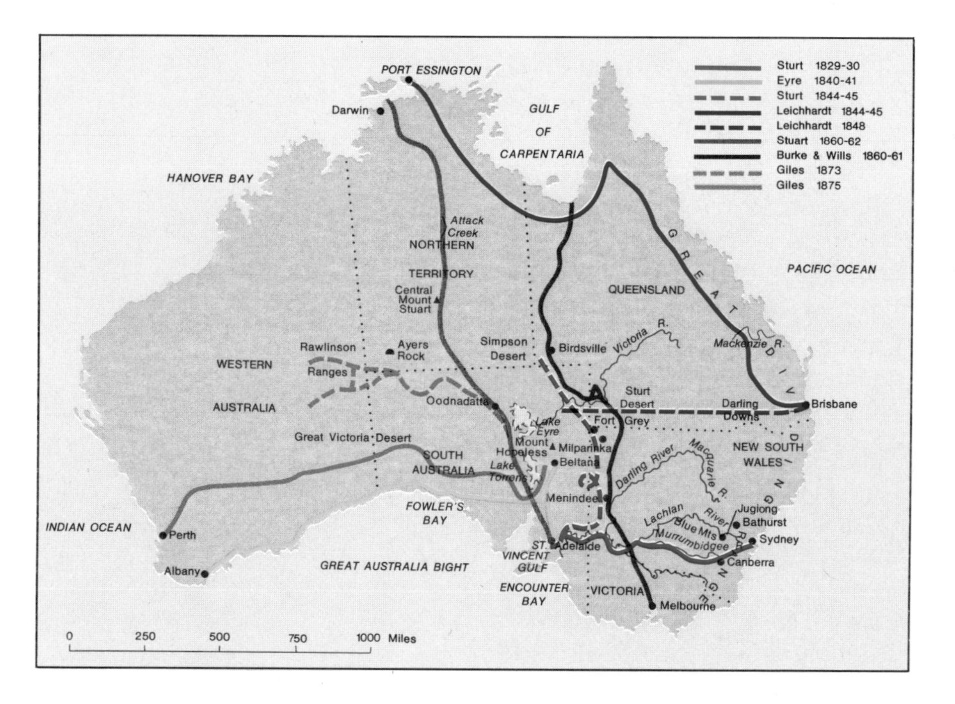

The map routes taken by the Outback explorers discussed in this book are traced on the map on the left. The men were tough and adventurous pioneers who, in spite of appalling hardships, opened up the interior of the continent while searching for new stock routes, arable lands, a mythical inland freshwater sea—and fame.

His new expedition started from Sydney on November 7, 1829, with a 27-foot whaleboat loaded in sections in a dray. Travelling south-westwards, the party reached the Murrumbidgee near Jugiong, where they set up camp and assembled the boat. On January 7, 1830, Sturt and seven other men set off in the boat down the Murrumbidgee on what was to become one of the epic journeys of Australian exploration. During the next 33 days they covered a thousand miles—rowing, sailing when the wind was favourable, or simply drifting with the current. They swept through rapids that merged with a new river, which Sturt named the Murray, and passed the confluence of the Darling. Finally they reached the end of the Murray. The river flowed, not into an inland sea as had been hoped, but into a small, land-locked lake within earshot of the surf in Encounter Bay, on Australia's southern coast, just east of the present site of Adelaide. Sturt had found the outlet of the river, but at terrible cost. The men were too weak to trek westwards across a low range of mountains to St. Vincent's Gulf, where they might have been able to pick up a ship to take them back to Sydney; and huge breakers blocked Encounter Bay from shipping. Nor were they equipped to make a return journey overland to Sydney: the only way back was the route by which they had come.

For eight weeks the men rowed upstream against the current. They were short of food and water, continually harassed by Aborigines, and their hands became raw with running sores. "Weak with poverty of diet," Sturt recorded, they frequently fell asleep at the oars. "The men lost the proper and muscular jerk with which they once made the waters foam and the oars bend, their arms appeared to be nerveless, their faces became haggard, their persons emaciated, their spirits wholly sunk." Incredibly, they managed to reach their base depot, where two men volunteered to go in search of help. They returned with a relief party to find Sturt handing out the last rations of flour. The expedition was escorted back to Sydney without mishap, but when Sturt finally reached civilization he went blind for several months, probably as a result of the continual glare off the river. In spite of his ordeal and the fact that he had solved the mystery of the rivers in the south-east, he clung to the belief in the inland sea. Some years later he was once again to search for that elusive and non-existent body of water.

In the 1830s settlements grew and prospered in south-east Australia, and a scattering of townships mushroomed along the coastal fringes of the continent. Sturt's favourable reports of the country he had explored led to the foundation of the province of South Australia in 1834. Only a few miles from where his expedition floundered to a halt, the town of Adelaide was built; with a large influx of settlers to the new province, it grew into a booming city by the end of the 1830s. Sturt's journey inspired other explorers to whittle away the edges of the unknown; but the blank in the middle of the map remained.

In 1840 an expedition was mounted in the young city of Adelaide to strike into the heart of the continent. The project was originally conceived to find an overland route for cattle drives along Australia's southern coast to new pastures and markets to the west; but the young man chosen to command the expedition, Edward Eyre, persuaded the sponsors that the idea was impractical. He had already probed by land along the Great Australian Bight as far as Streaky Bay, about 300 miles west of Adelaide, and found only waterless scrubland. No cattle could move that way, he said; why not go north, into the Centre, to see what lay up there? The sponsors agreed.

Eyre, the son of a Yorkshire clergyman, had emigrated to Australia at the age of 17 and, although he was only 24 when asked to lead the expedition, he was already a respected bushman with his own cattle station north of Adelaide. In June 1840, he galloped out of Adelaide accompanied by only five companions and two Aborigines. It was, contemporary accounts recorded, a "heart-stirring and inspiring scene". Eyre carried with him a Union Jack, sewn by the ladies of the city and given to him by Sturt, who told him to carry it "to the centre of the continent, there to leave it as a sign to the savage that the footsteps of civilized men had penetrated so far".

Unfortunately, only 400 miles north of Adelaide, the expedition was halted by an expanse of salt marshes between Lake Torrens, which he named, and another salt lake that 18 years later would be given his name. The white crust of the marshes gave way and the horses sank to their bellies in clinging mud. Mirages added to Eyre's difficulties. "From the extraordinary and deceptive appearances caused by mirage and refraction," he wrote, "it was impossible to tell what to make of sensible objects, or what to believe on the evidence of vision."

Eyre abandoned the march north. Bitterly disappointed and determined to find a way of "making amends for past failure", he sent word back to Adelaide that he intended to revert to the plan he had dismissed originally: he would head south-west down to Fowler's Bay, on the Great Australian Bight, then strike west for a thousand miles along the coast to Albany, in Western Australia. Eyre made the 300-mile journey to Fowler's Bay, then set out with only one white man and three Aborigines on a trek that was to erupt in murder. In extreme heat, tortured by blood-sucking flies, the little band plodded on, day after day, eventually dumping some of their guns and ammunition, saddles and coats to lighten their loads. After 60 days, close to starvation, they were forced to eat one of their horses and collect dew to drink. Then, a month later, two of the Aborigines, convinced that the expedition was doomed, shot dead Eyre's white overseer and fled with the remaining guns, ammunition and most of the food. "The frightful, the appalling truth now burst upon me, that I was alone in this desert," Eyre wrote in his journal. "At the dead hour of night in the wildest and most inhospitable wastes of Australia, with the fierce wind raging in unison with the scene of violence before me, I was left with a single native, whose fidelity I could not rely upon, and for aught I knew might be in league with the other two, who perhaps were even now lurking about with the view of taking away my life." But the third Aborigine proved loyal to the end. He and Eyre toiled along the coast for another 30 days until, 280 miles short of the port of Albany, they chanced on a French whaler, captained by an Englishman, anchored just offshore. After resting on board for a few days, they finished their journey. It was an

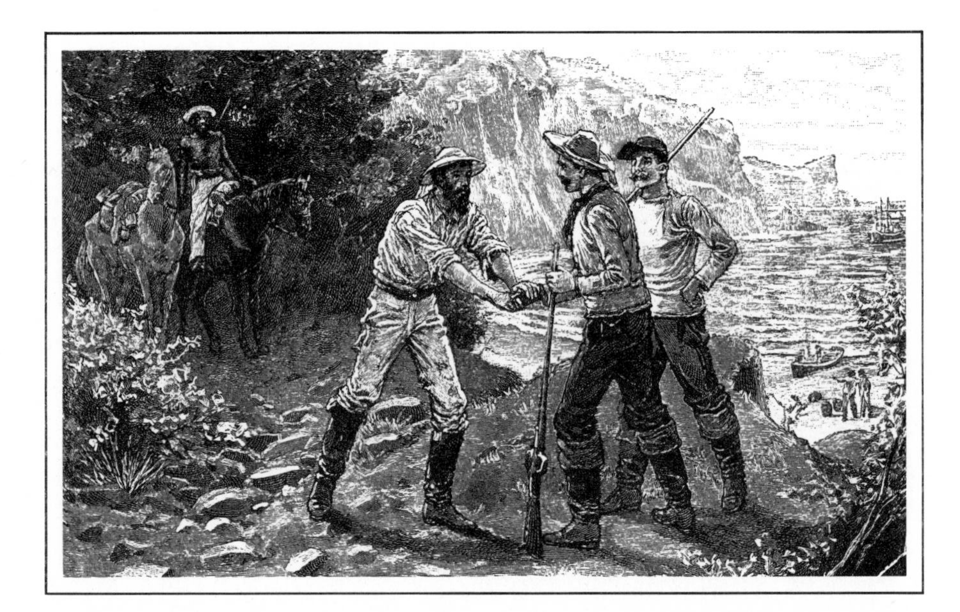

At the end of his strength after trekking 700 miles west along the south coast in 1841, Edward Eyre greets sailors who had seen his signals for help from their anchored whaler. Eyre had started from Adelaide in search of a stock route to Western Australia. He had failed in that goal, but went on to complete an epic 1,000-mile journey to Albany, surviving heat, thirst and an attack by Aborigines in his party.

ordeal that established little except Eyre's courage; he had failed to find a way westwards through the Centre, and he proved only what he had always suspected—that there was no practicable route for cattle to Western Australia around the Bight.

Fifteen years after his first expedition, Captain Sturt, at 49, was still dreaming of finding an inland sea. In 1844 he made another attempt to discover the fabled body of water—this time in the wastes of the Centre. The expedition left Adelaide in August 1844, with 16 men, 30 bullocks and 200 sheep on the hoof, four drays and a section-built boat with which to sail on the inland sea. They first struck east, up the Murray and Darling rivers, to avoid the salt marshes that had blocked Eyre, then turned north-west across a stony, drought-stricken plain. Daytime temperatures soared well over 100° F. as they pressed on through "salty spinifex and sand ridges, driving for hundreds of miles into the very heart of the interior as if they would never end". Sturt recorded one experience that approached a scene from a medieval allegory. Several hundred kites swooped down on his party to see if they were some new kind of prey, flapping away only at the last moment, "opening their beaks and spreading their talons . . . too numerous for us to have overpowered if they had really attacked us".

In January, Sturt and his men reached a creek site with permanent water near Milparinka. They called it Depot Creek, and there they were to be marooned for six months by drought; for reconnaissance forays could find no water ahead, and the waterholes they had already passed had dried up, thus cutting off their retreat. The temperatures steadily increased, sometimes reaching as much as 157° F. They dug an underground room in an attempt to escape the heat, but still suffered. "Our hair, as well as the wool on our sheep, ceased to grow," Sturt wrote, "and our nails had become brittle as glass." In April the scorching summer months gave way to the bitter cold of winter, when the mercury dropped to only 24° F. But still no rain fell. The men suffered from scurvy. James Poole, the expedition's second-in-command, turned black and his mouth became so badly festered that he could hardly eat. He died on July 16, four days after the onset of the rains that were to liberate the group from their disease-ridden camp.

Sturt also had scurvy, but he was determined to continue to the north, still convinced that up there lay the inland sea. The expedition trekked onwards for another 80 miles to a new campsite, which Sturt named Fort Grey. In August 1845, leaving his boat with the order that it should be painted and prepared for launching, he set off on horseback with four other men on a final push into the interior. Extra pack horses carried 15 weeks' provisions. At first they made good progress, but soon they were in a stony desert (now called the Sturt Desert) where the sun had opened deep fissures in the ground. In some places, Sturt recorded, "there was scarcely room for the horses to tread, and they kept constantly slipping their hind feet into chasms from eight to ten feet deep, into which the earth fell with a hollow rumbling sound, as into a grave".

Still they pressed on, mile after mile, until at last they reached the southern edge of the Simpson Desert, still 400 miles from the centre of the continent. There, Sturt was forced to halt. "From the summit of a sandy undulation close upon our right," he wrote, "we saw that the ridges extended northwards in parallel lines beyond the range of vision, and appeared as if interminable. To the eastward and westward they succeeded each other like the waves of the sea. The sand was of a deep red colour, and a bright narrow line of it marked the top of each ridge, amidst the sickly pink and glaucous coloured vegetation around .... My companion involuntarily uttered an exclamation of amazement when he first glanced his eye over it. 'Good Heavens,' said he, 'did ever man see such country!' "

Sturt and his party fell back on Fort Grey, only to find the camp deserted and red, foul water in the creek. The other members of the party had given Sturt up for dead, and had retreated the 80 miles to

Depot Creek with the expedition's livestock. Nevertheless, after a few days' rest Sturt and his small team again rode north in search of the sea, and reached a point near the present site of Birdsville before progress was once more halted by the dunes of the Simpson. Sturt was now grievously ill, and this time he conceded defeat. His party made a forced march south to Depot Creek, where they caught up with the rest of the expedition. Sturt was in too much agony to ride or walk the 118 miles to the next water. After dumping his boat at last and ordering five bullocks to be killed so that their hides could be filled with water, he had himself placed on a dray, and in this manner he slowly, painfully made the long journey back from the desert that had beaten him.

It was Sturt's last expedition, and thereafter no one held out any hopes of finding an inland sea; but there were many parts of inland Australia left to explore and plenty of hopeful explorers. Not all of them had the persistence and fortitude of Sturt. Perhaps the most controversial of them was Ludwig Leichhardt, a blundering Prussian eccentric who made his name in 1845 with a 3,000-mile journey from Darling Downs, in eastern Queensland, to Port Essington, on the north coast, in search of new grazing lands.

Leichhardt had left his home in Germany to avoid military service and arrived in Australia in 1842, hoping to get a scientific job with the government of New South Wales. When that did not materialize, he borrowed off friends for a couple of years until he heard that an expedition was being planned to look for new farming territory and navigable rivers and harbours north of Queensland. There was a dispute over who should lead the expedition and, while it was being sorted out, Leichhardt persuaded a group of businessmen to sponsor him as the leader of a private expedition with the same objective.

He set out from Darling Downs in October 1844, and soon proved he was both a poor bushman and a poor leader of men. Only a few days out, the expedition lost 143 pounds of flour when Leichhardt led the way into a dense thicket of scrub that tore the bags from the backs of the bullocks. Much of the time he had no idea where he was. His navigation was so inept that on one occasion he "fixed" the party's position at a point 20 miles out at sea. Nor did he take any precautions against hostile Aboriginal tribes; as a result his men were asleep, with guns unloaded, when a shower of spears fell into their camp near the Mitchell river in northern Queensland. The naturalist John Gilbert was killed and two other members of the party, John Roper and James Calvert, were severely beaten and wounded. "Several of these spears were barbed,"

Leichhardt recorded, "and could not be extracted without difficulty. I had to force one through the arm of Roper, to break off the barb; and to cut another out of the groin of Mr. Calvert."

The expedition lost more equipment as it straggled northwards, and morale plummeted; one of the Aboriginal porters, threatened with discipline for taking time off to hunt possums and look for honey, punched Leichhardt in the mouth, dislodging two teeth. Leichhardt himself hardly set an admirable example: he wolfed down whatever food he could lay his hands on, including a particularly obnoxious-smelling dingo and many flying foxes ("They are very fat, particularly between the shoulders and on the rump . . . most delicate eating.") In spite of Leichhardt's poor leadership and the death of his naturalist, the expedition was an undoubted success, for Leichhardt and his men discovered thousands of acres of good grazing country and many new rivers. When they stumbled into Port Essington on the northern coast in December 1845, more than a year after their departure from Darling Downs and long after they had been presumed dead, they found themselves national heroes and collected awards totalling £2,500.

Leichhardt's second expedition, 12 months later, however, was a fiasco. His plan was to make a transcontinental trek across Australia from Sydney to Perth. He kept no record of the journey, but his men scribbled diaries that drew their own lurid picture. John Mann, a surveyor with the expedition, claimed that Leichhardt delayed the start by stampeding the cattle and goats, walking among them at night "so they could become accustomed to his presence". When the men came down with fever near the Mackenzie river, they discovered that their leader had forgotten to bring sufficient medicine. Leichhardt claimed they got sick through over-eating, yet when he had a touch of fever himself, his companions had a melodramatic hypochondriac on their hands. "Bury me," he gasped, "in a spot that can readily be recognized." When he was fit again he took charge of the emergency rations, cooking meals for himself at night while the sick went without. At the Mackenzie river in Queensland, the expedition broke up with much bitter quarrelling and the men returned to Sydney.

News of what happened quickly spread, and self-respecting bushmen refused to join Leichhardt when, in 1848, he started recruiting for a third expedition—another attempt at an east-west transcontinental crossing. Nevertheless, the bombastic explorer was determined to place his reputation beyond doubt. He obtained two inexperienced Europeans, two hired labourers (one an ex-convict) and two Aborigines, and in April 1848, started out from Queensland in the direction of the Centre. The seven men were never seen again.

The disappearance of the expedition is one of the great mysteries of Australian exploration. Not a trace of Leichhardt, his companions or his equipment has ever been found. Their bones may lie in the Simpson Desert, directly on Leichhardt's route west, for nowhere else, surely, could so many skeletons and bullock-carts moulder without being discovered. Searchers at first thought that the expedition must have died of thirst and that their remains had been buried under a deluge of mud caused by a flash-flood. In 1852 Aborigines claimed they had massacred the party when some of its members molested native women, but not a shred of hard evidence surfaced. Leichhardt relics, Leichhardt skeletons appeared everywhere—there was even a Ladies' Leichhardt Expedition in 1865, equipped by the ladies of Victoria, to investigate the letter L carved upon an Outback tree. Many people refused to believe that Leichhardt was dead. Dozens of search parties went out during ensuing decades, chasing rumours of a crazed white man who lived with the natives. As recently as 1953 an expedition from Perth searched the Rawlinson Ranges in Western Australia for a mysterious iron box—believed to be Leichhardt's medicine chest or his personal treasure of gold sovereigns—that was reputed to be in the area. The Aborigines, it was said, did not dare to open it. The chest was never found.

John McDouall Stuart, who arrived at the centre of Australia on April 22, 1860, marks his achievement by displaying the British flag. But his attempt to press on to the north coast had to be abandoned in the face of hunger and harassment by Aborigines. A few months later, sickness and exhaustion defeated his second bid to complete a south-north crossing of the continent. Not until his third try, in July, 1862, did he reach the north coast—only to learn that another expedition had beaten him to it.

By 1850 the Centre was still an enigma—a barrier that effectively cut off the southern, settled part of the continent from the north. In 1860 the South Australian government offered a bounty of £2,000 to the first expedition to cross Australia from south to north. The offer was not motivated entirely by a desire to discover what lay at the heart of the continent; the government also wanted to find a route along which it could establish a telegraph link-up between its capital, Adelaide, and the port of Darwin. The neighbouring state of Victoria immediately responded with a similar challenge, and a transcontinental race was on.

Two men rose to the challenge—John McDouall Stuart in Adelaide, and Robert O'Hara Burke in Melbourne. They were very different characters. Stuart, at 45, was a tough, dour Scot and an experienced explorer who had served as a draughtsman on Captain Charles Sturt's last expedition. Burke, at 39, was a big, black-bearded, romantic Irishman who had chased excitement all his life, as soldier, gold miner and police inspector; he was also, rumour had it, anxious to impress a beautiful young actress. Stuart's expedition was privately financed and modestly equipped, whereas Burke's was lavishly sponsored by the Royal Society of Victoria to the amount of £12,000.

Stuart got away first, in March 1860, accompanied by only two other men and 13 horses. The little group made astonishing progress. They headed north-west to avoid the salt marshes around Lake Eyre and then due north into the centre of the continent. On April 22 Stuart calculated by the sun that he had reached the long-sought-for goal—the geographical centre of Australia. He climbed a near-by hill, which he named Central Mount Sturt in honour of his former leader, and planted a Union Jack on its summit. The hill was later renamed Central Mount Stuart in his honour. Then, hardly waiting to savour his triumph, he pressed on, travelling northwards for a time without mishap except when he was thrown by his horse and dragged some way through the scrub with his ankle caught in a stirrup. But at a place that Stuart named Attack Creek, about 350 miles north of the present site of Alice Springs, the party ran into a hostile tribe of Aborigines and were forced to turn back. The return journey took them more than three months; they arrived back in Adelaide in October to learn that the Burke expedition had left Melbourne with much ceremony two months earlier.

In November the indomitable Stuart, still hoping to beat Burke to the north coast, set off again, retracing his own tracks. Once again he crossed the Centre and trekked a hundred miles past Attack Creek, only to be stopped this time by a wilderness of dense scrub that ripped clothes and packs to shreds. In addition he and his men were stricken with scurvy, dysentery and sheer exhaustion. They could go no farther. Back they trekked to Adelaide, which they reached in September 1861. There they learned that the Burke expedition was long overdue and that search parties were trying to locate it.

But Stuart did not wait to hear of the fate of Burke's expedition. Just one month later he set out for a third attempt to cross the continent and this time he was to succeed. On July 24, 1862 he arrived on the northern shores of Australia, east of Darwin, and gazed out across the Indian Ocean. "I advanced a few yards on to the beach," Stuart wrote, "and was gratified and delighted to find the waters of the Indian Ocean . . . before the party with the horses knew anything of its proximity. Thring, who rode in advance of me, called out 'The sea!' which took them all by surprise, and they were so astonished that he had to repeat his call before they fully understand what was meant. Then they immediately gave three long and hearty cheers."

Their excitement was short lived. They faced an horrific return journey—2,000 miles back the way they had just come. Stuart again went down with scurvy and could ride no farther. Racked by fits of coughing and half blind, he was carried on a litter slung between two horses. But still he kept his diary. "I feel in the grip of death," he wrote on October 31. "My right hand is useless. I am totally blind after sunset." In December the men tottered into Adelaide looking like scarecrows, without even the satisfaction of having won the race to the north coast. For they learned that although Burke was dead, his expedition had reached the Gulf of Carpentaria in February.

Burke's expedition was to go down in history not only as the first to make a crossing of Australia from south to north, but also as one of the most rashly conducted of them all. The expedition consisted of 17 men, about 25 camels, 22 horses and a string of special carts to carry supplies and equipment. No expense had been spared; the men had even been kitted out in a special "uniform": scarlet jumpers, flannel trousers and broad-rimmed hats. But the send-off ceremony in Melbourne, which thousands of cheering citizens attended, was hardly over before quarrels began. Burke, although courageous, was no bushman; he was a quick-tempered, ham-fisted, impetuous man with a gift for precisely the wrong decision—and worse, he was unlucky. His brusque manner caused two men to quit even before a base camp had been established at Menindee on the Darling river, south of the present town of Broken Hill.

From Menindee, Burke led an advance party on to a second camp at Cooper's Creek. There he waited for the rest of the expedition to join him, seething with impatience, sweltering in the heat and pestered by flies. After five weeks he decided he could wait no longer: he had made up his mind to "dash into the interior and cross the continent at all hazards". On December 16, 1860, he mounted his grey charger, Billy, and headed northwards, with William Wills, John King and Charlie Gray behind him on camels, and enough supplies for three months. The five men left behind were ordered to wait at Cooper's Creek for four months or until their supplies were exhausted.

The journey started well. Even the natives they met on the way were friendly. "They gave us fish and offered their women," Burke recorded. On the final stages he travelled ahead with Wills, and together the two men hacked their way through miles of mangrove swamp until, on February 11, 1861, after a journey totalling more than 1,500 miles, they reached the Gulf of Carpentaria on Australia's northern coast. Standing

John King, sole survivor of the team that made the first south-north crossing of Australia, weeps beside the body of Robert Burke, the expedition leader. Having reached the north coast in February, 1861, King, Burke and his deputy, William Wills, returned to their depot at Cooper's Creek only hours after it had been abandoned by the base party, who had given the explorers up for dead. Too weak to travel farther, Burke and Wills slowly starved, but King was cared for by Aborigines until his rescue in September 1861.

ankle deep in mud that stained their boots and trousers with salt, they solemnly shook hands, then returned to join Gray and King. Time was short: the 700-mile trek from Cooper's Creek had taken them eight weeks, and only five weeks' food remained to sustain them on their journey back. Burke picked up dysentery and Gray became terribly ill. At first the others accused Gray of slacking, but on April 17 he died. The food soon ran short. They gnawed sticks of dried meat and, when that ran out, they ate the grey charger. At last, on April 21, they staggered into Cooper's Creek, to find the camp deserted. The base party had pulled out only seven hours before, according to a letter they had left behind. To suffer for so long and miss salvation by only a few hours! Black despair filled the men. Weak and exhausted though they were, Wills wanted to try and overtake the retreating base party, but Burke refused and insisted that they should follow Cooper's Creek south towards aptly named Mount Hopeless, seeking help from pioneers who had settled there. It was a mistake.

"To whom it may concern," Burke wrote. "We proceed on, tomorrow, slowly down the creek towards Adelaide. . . . We have suffered much from hunger. . . . We are greatly disappointed at finding the party here gone." They buried the letter neatly, smoothing over the earth to prevent Aborigines from digging it up, but mystifyingly they left no mark to show they had returned. Their journey proved hopeless. They ate their camels—reduced to bones and gristle mostly—and sometimes fish and nardoo, a paste of pounded seeds, provided by Aborigines whom Burke, not wanting to get too friendly with them, scared off by shooting over their heads. But they grew weaker all the time and abandoned any idea of reaching Mount Hopeless.

Meanwhile, the base party had met a group bringing up more supplies. Smitten by conscience, the men decided to ride back to Cooper's Creek on the off-chance that Burke's party might have returned. But they found the camp just as they had left it and turned their horses back to the south, unaware that their companions were only a few miles away, close to death. Towards the end of June, Wills—cool and brave to the end—persuaded Burke and King to leave him in a shelter constructed from branches while they sought help. Wills knew he was going to die. "Nothing now but the greatest good luck can save any of us," he wrote in his diary, "and as for myself I may live four or five days if the weather continues warm. My pulse is at forty-eight, and very weak, and my legs and arms are nearly skin and bone. I can only look out, like Mr. Micawber, 'for something to turn up'; but starvation on nardoo is by no means unpleasant."

Burke and King staggered on for only a few miles—Burke in pain, King exhorting him to keep going. Burke scrawled in his notebook: "I hope we shall be done justice to. We have fulfilled our task, but we have been aban - - - " His final entry read: "King has behaved nobly. He has stayed with me to the last, and placed the pistol in my hand, leaving me lying on the surface as I wished. R. O'Hara Burke. Cooper's Creek, June 28th." He died next morning at about 8 o'clock. "I felt very lonely", wrote King. He shot three crows for food and returned to the shelter where Wills had been left, only to find him dead, too. He followed the Aborigines and linked up with them, helping around their camp as best he could. For their part, they took pity on this human scarecrow and gave him food and somewhere to sleep. Wasted to a shadow and dressed in rags, he wandered with the natives until a search party found him in September 1861. The Burke and Wills expedition was over, with bitter charges and recriminations to come.

It had been a model of how not to explore Australia—tragic and futile. Burke took few notes, and the various expeditions mounted to rescue his party contributed far more to a knowledge of the interior than the dead heroes did. Even Burke's route was useless for the future. Had it not been for the extraordinarily wet season of 1860-61, Burke's desperate beeline for the coast would have killed his party long before they returned to Cooper's Creek. When the Overland Telegraph to Darwin was built in 1872, it followed almost exactly the alternative line of Stuart's march, with its well-planned stages and permanent water.

The Burke and Wills fiasco marked the end of large-scale expeditions into the interior. If nothing else, their journey had proved that there was little hope of discovering land in the interior suitable for colonization. As the Melbourne *Argus* pointed out in December 1862: "The successful discoveries reported within the year now ending leave little more for the explorer to do in Australia." That assessment was not entirely true. In the wake of the explorers there came pioneers of a different kind—prospectors, mineralogists and naturalists, who have since been unravelling the mysteries of Australia's complex geology and natural history. But the Ghastly Blank of the Centre had been largely filled in, and only the detailed work remained.

Perhaps that is why Ernest Giles, who made his inland journeys in the 1870s, never received the acclaim accorded to the earlier explorers. In 1876 he wrote: "The history of Australian exploration, though not yet quite complete, is now so advanced towards its end that only minor details are wanting to fill the volume up; and though I shall not attempt to rank myself among the first, or the greatest, yet I think I have reason to call myself the last, of the Australian explorers." He was more than that: he was the last worthy member of a fanatical brotherhood who, in his words, "passed through a baptism worse, indeed, than that of fire—the baptism of no water".

Pioneer Naturalists in the Outback

On May 6, 1894, a band of men mounted on camels struck out northwards from the Outback township of Oodnadatta. The men were members of the Horn Scientific Expedition, and their goal was the Macdonnell Ranges of central Australia, which were a source of intrigue to 19th-Century naturalists. Early visitors had reported that the mountains formed an oasis in the surrounding deserts, prompting speculation that they might harbour species from a time when Australia was wetter and cooler. The Expedition intended finding out whether this was so.

Shortly after leaving Oodnadatta, the party traversed a desert. Water was scarce, but the expedition located some by following flocks of birds to springs. A more unusual problem was posed by the camels. They were hardy beasts of burden, conceded the expedition zoologist, Baldwin Spencer, but from the viewpoint of a specimen collector they were exasperating. "You may often see, say, a lizard or an insect which you are anxious to secure," Spencer complained, "but long before you can persuade your camel to sit down the animal is far away."

By the beginning of July the expedition was encamped deep in the Macdonnells. The scientists' first reaction was one of disappointment, for as Spencer recorded, they found "no great sheltered valleys or luxuriant vegetation". They swallowed their disappointment and began collecting and identifying animal specimens. This, too, proved frustrating at first, because they unearthed only a "monotonous and small series of animals". Then rain fell, and in the following days a hitherto hidden wildlife appeared as if by magic. "Insects formerly unseen come about in swarms," wrote Spencer, "caterpillars in thousands creep about, the majority of them simply falling prey to the lizards and birds which increase with like rapidity."

From among this throng the naturalists collected 171 new species. Although these were not the hoped-for survivors of Australia's more fertile past, they had a fascination all their own. The remarkable feature of the fauna, concluded Spencer, was its ability to thrive in arid conditions. The naturalists' notes on the animals' survival techniques were pioneering studies in desert ecology. Their work was illustrated with painstakingly drawn plates, some of which are reproduced on the following pages.

A bird of arid scrubland, the princess parrot is a nomadic seed-eater that was sighted only once by the Horn Expedition. "The fact of so few being seen," wrote the ornithologist, Alfred North, "may be due to the singular habit the bird has of lying along the stout limbs of the trees like a lizard."

Horn Expd. Cent. Aust. Zoology Plate 5
N. Cayley del. Troedel & C° Print.
R. Wendel Lith. Melbourne

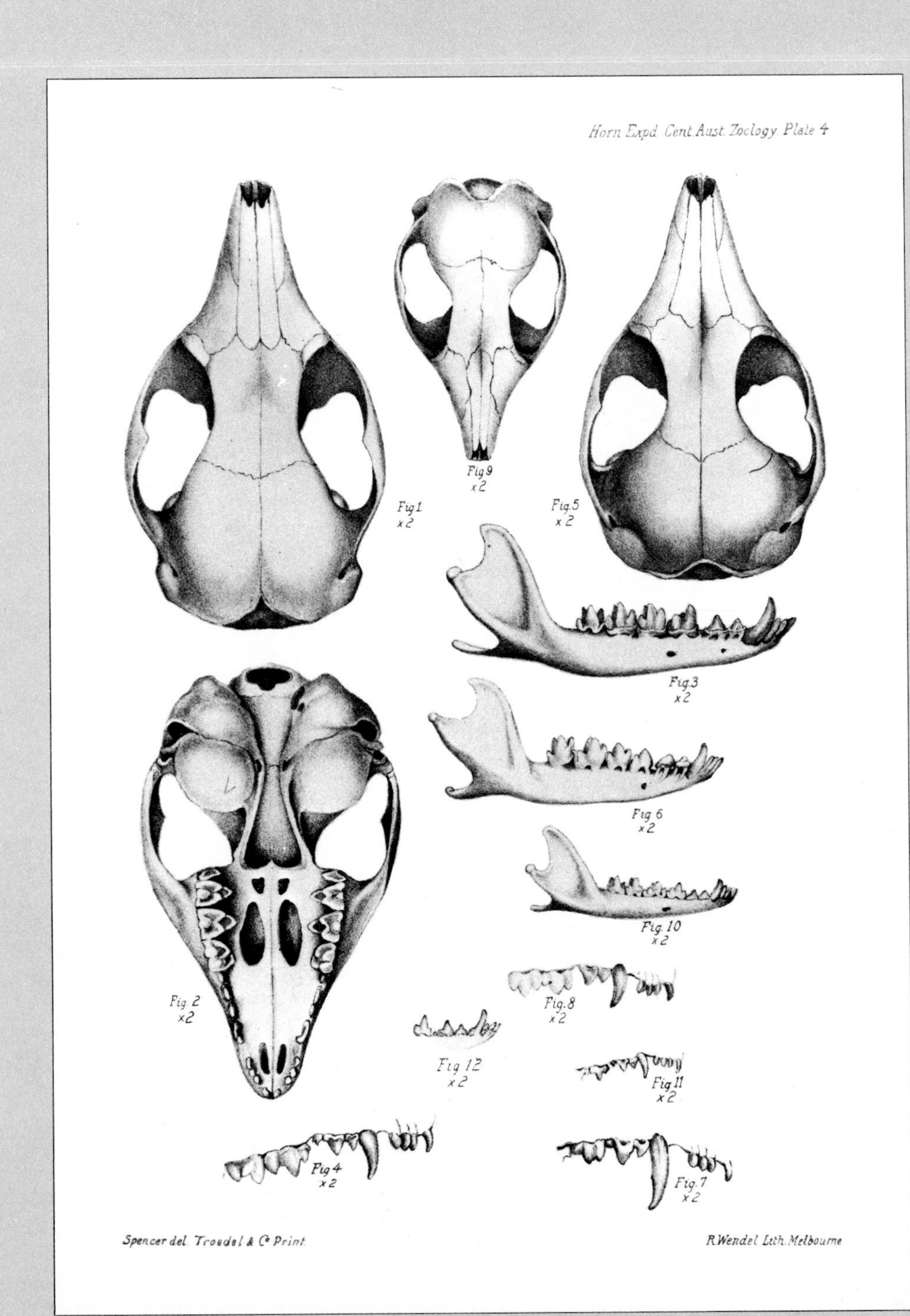

SKULLS AND JAWBONES OF MARSUPIAL "MICE"

Small Nocturnal Hunters

Among the scientific prizes brought back by the Horn Expedition were five previously unknown species of marsupial "mice", two of which are shown life-size on the right.

These marsupials are not rodents nor are they mouselike in behaviour; they are, in fact, little, pouch-bearing carnivores with needle-sharp teeth. While some, like the stripe-faced dunnart (right, Fig. 2), eat spiders and grasshoppers, others prey on larger game—lizards, birds and true mice. Most hunt at night and hide from the heat of the day.

Collecting these elusive creatures was not easy. Although Spencer offered Aborigines he met "a shirt and a lot of tobacco" for capturing the red-eared antechinus (right, Fig. 1), which can survive in lean times on the fat stored in its bulging tail, he acquired only two specimens.

Keeping specimens in the field was difficult—they deteriorated rapidly in the heat unless pickled as soon as killed—and identifying them was even harder. Distinctions between species were often made by analysing minute variations of shape and colouring—which is why Spencer was unhappy to learn that a mounted example of a known species he used for comparison had been patched up with bits of skin from other animals. Faced with such difficulties, Spencer made some mistakes in classification which later were rectified by other zoologists; but mostly his descriptions were models of detail and accuracy.

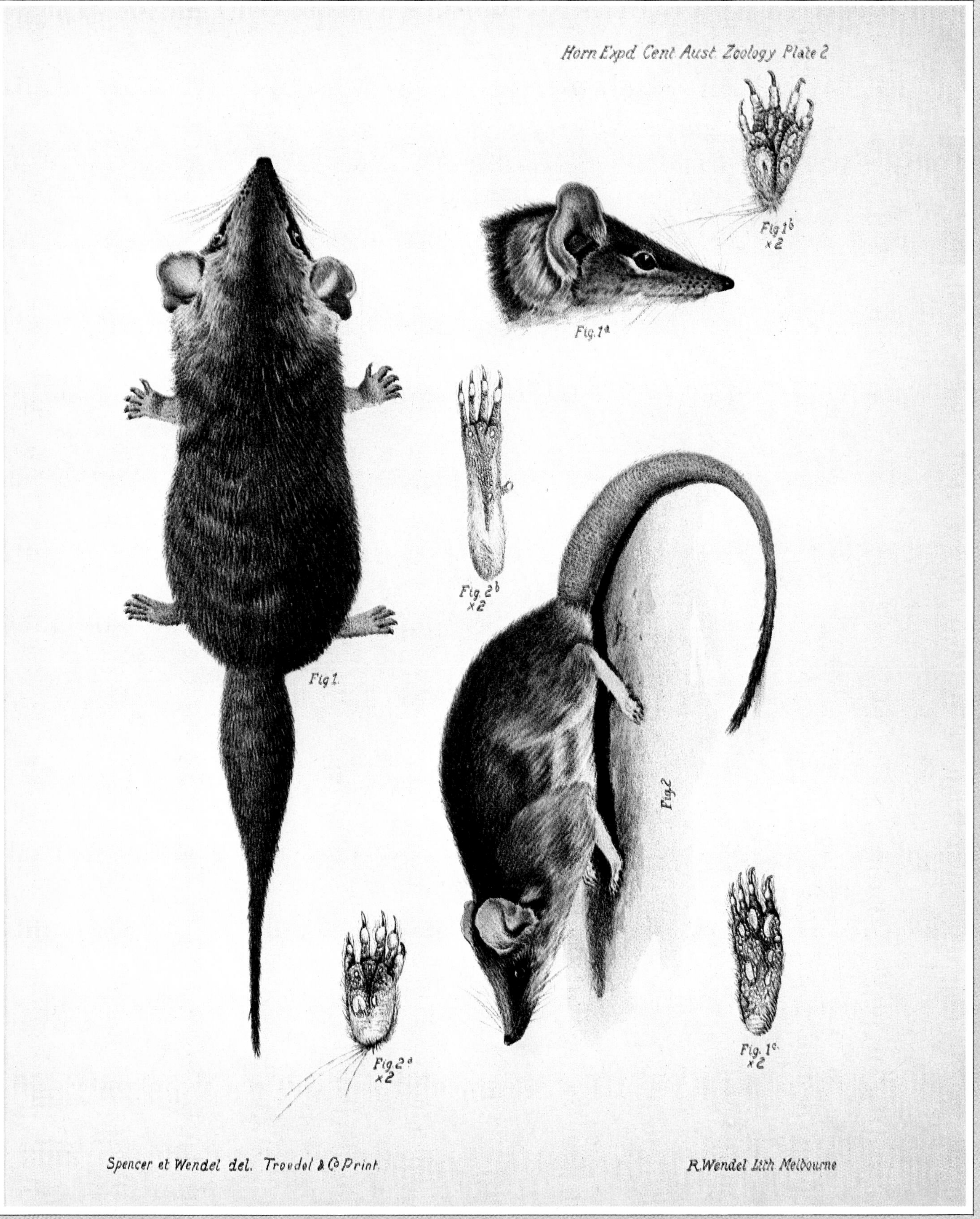

SPECIMENS OF RED-EARED ANTECHINUS (FIG. 1) AND STRIPE-FACED DUNNART (FIG. 2)

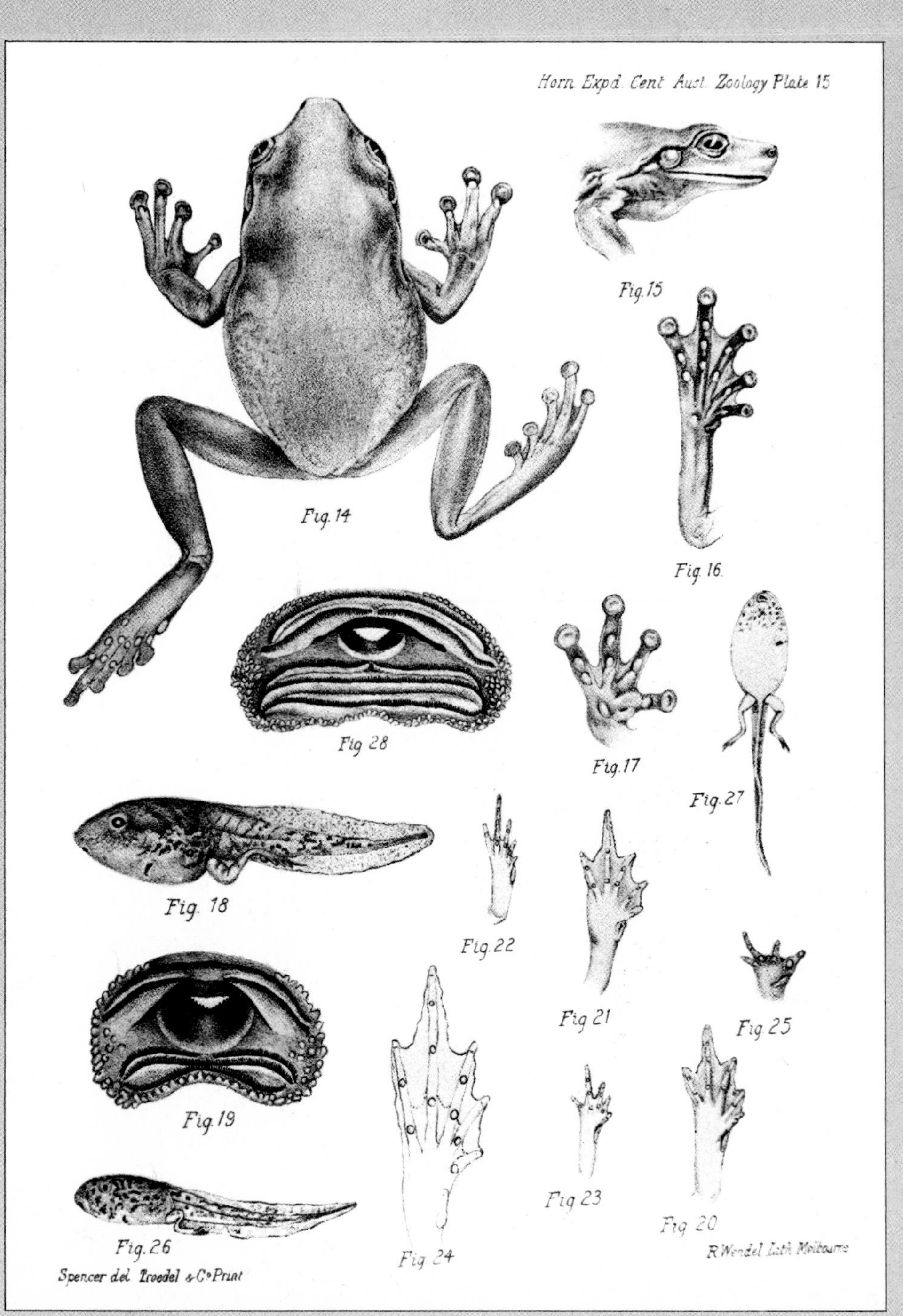

ANATOMICAL DRAWINGS OF OUTBACK FROGS. FIGS. 19 AND 28 SHOW TADPOLE MOUTHS

Living Water-bottles

Travelling in the dry season, the members of the Horn Expedition were surprised to find a thriving population of frogs in the Outback, even in places where no rain had fallen for more than two years. The zoologist Baldwin Spencer reasoned that the frogs must either have abandoned their amphibious mode of life or evolved habits that enabled them to survive drought until there was enough water in which eggs and tadpoles could develop.

The latter explanation proved correct. Immediately after downpours frogs such as the water-holding frog (right, Fig. 1) and the moaning frog (right, Fig. 2) were found in abundance around the waterholes, their normally drab colours brightened. The colour changes were a prelude to mating, the scientists realized. Within days of a rainstorm the pools were swarming with tadpoles, which developed much faster than those in wetter regions. The new generation of frogs had reached maturity before the creeks and pools dried up.

Having established that the frogs were opportunist breeders, the scientists investigated some of the methods by which the amphibians survived drought. Guided by Aborigines, the scientists found frogs such as the ornate burrowing frog (right, Figs. 3 and 4) hidden in deep, cool tunnels, their bodies swollen with water to tide them over to the next rains. When the frogs were examined, they were seen to have broad, strong toes (left) for digging.

COLOURFUL AND STRIKINGLY PATTERNED OUTBACK FROGS SWOLLEN WITH WATER

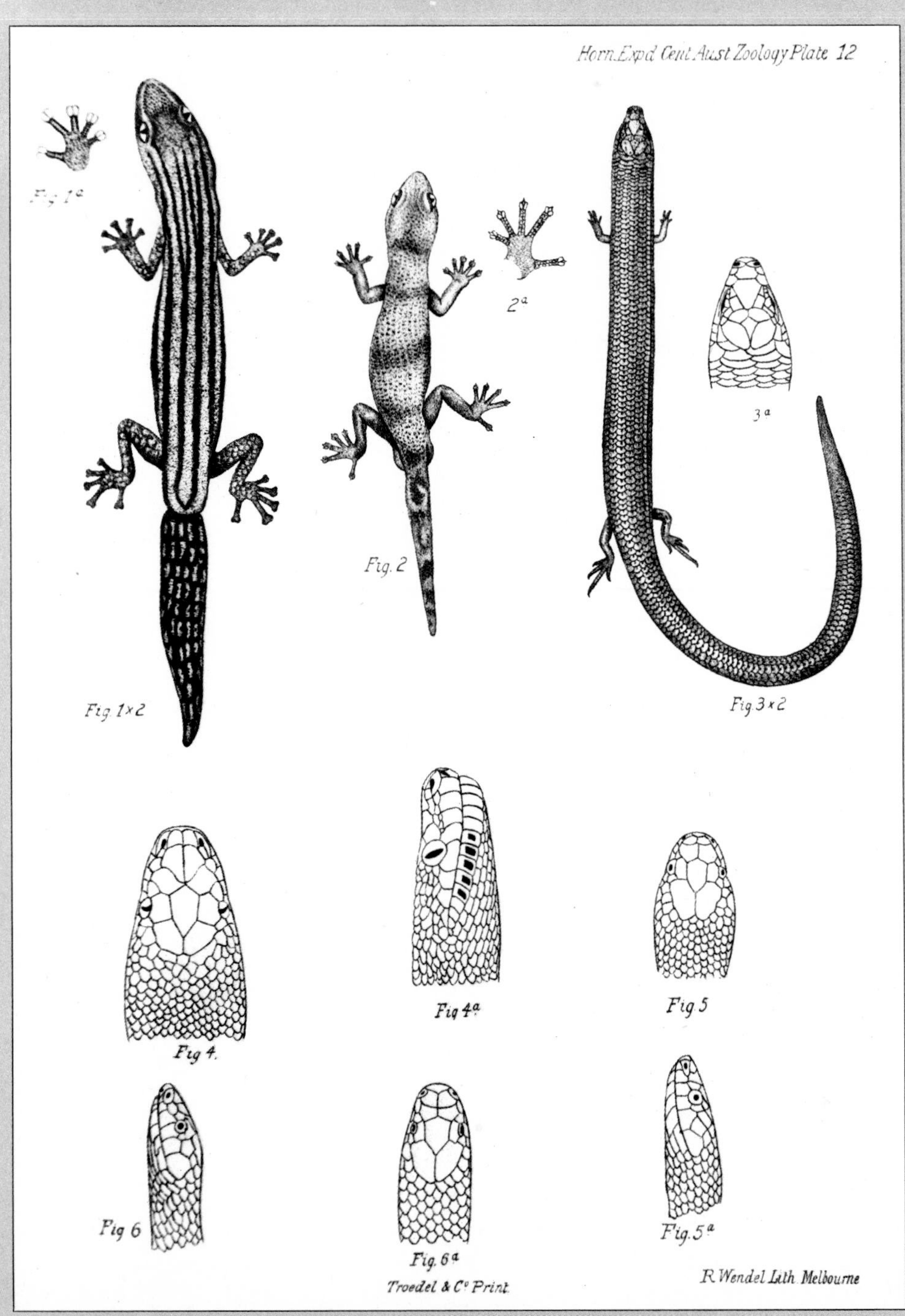

LIZARDS (TOP AND CENTRE) AND HEADS OF SNAKES (BOTTOM)

A Wealth of Reptiles

Reptiles, found in abundance by the Expedition, responded to downpours in much the same way as frogs. After rain, Spencer recorded, lizards became more active and grew fat on caterpillars. Their drab, dry-season colours brightened to gaudy hues like those on the right, and mating began. At such times collecting was easy, but in dry periods the naturalists sometimes had to burn brush in order to flush specimens.

The expedition gathered examples of 54 reptile species—12 of them new—including the painted dragon (right, Fig. 1); skinks with legs so tiny that they look like snakes (left, Fig. 3); and several true snakes.

Collecting reptiles had its risks. There are more than 70 kinds of poisonous snake in Australia and the Aborigines were not always reliable authorities on which species were dangerous. But the peril from snakes was probably no greater than that of flash-floods surging down stream-beds, nor more disturbing than harassment by stinging flies, which compelled the men to wrap their heads in muslin while working.

The expedition's hardships were equalled by its satisfactions, including one exclusive to naturalists: the privilege of naming new species. An otherwise obscure telegraph operator who helped the scientists, P. M. Byrne, was rewarded with a kind of immortality when his name was given to two animals—a lizard, *Diplodactylis byrnei* (left, Fig. 2), and a marsupial, *Dasyuroides byrnei*.

LIZARDS IN THEIR MATING-SEASON COLOURS

7/ The Flinders' Past Uncovered

I felt a new world had been opened up to me, and I had come into contact with the "bones of Nature" laid bare.

SIR HANS HEYSEN QUOTED BY HANS MINCHAM/ *THE STORY OF THE FLINDERS RANGES*

Our travels by aircraft over the Centre had given us some nerve-wracking moments—enough, at least, to make us grip our seats when Alison expertly slipped the aeroplane through updrafts of hot air over lonely desert landings. We had dozed occasionally, only to jerk awake as we plunged sickeningly down through what felt like holes in the sky. At other times, it seemed as though we were locked into one of those ping-pong balls that are perched on a column of air in a sales display: at any moment someone might flip a switch and down we would go. Our radio had been giving us trouble; and sometimes it would crackle and whistle as if with malice, blotting out the voices that tried periodically to reach us. At such moments only Alison understood the blurred messages coming through the ether. She would listen quietly and then reply with a clipped economy of response we all found reassuring. At other times, quite suddenly, the shrieking static would resolve itself into a welcome human voice addressing India Alpha Hotel, our call sign, as warm and close as though the radio operator were sitting in the cabin with us.

By the time we left Ayers Rock on the last stage of our travels, the little aeroplane cabin had become our familiar home, cluttered with maps, binoculars, notebooks and all the other paraphernalia of our Outback journey. We were heading south-east to the southern fringe of the Centre, flying 700 miles over sand dunes, scrub and saltflats towards the Flinders Ranges of South Australia. The Flinders, which start at

Crystal Brook in the south, extend for more than 250 miles to the arid plain south-east of Lake Eyre, and rise like a rugged pink headland from the desert sea. We had flown over the ranges before, between Broken Hill and Leigh Creek, but had seen them only from a distance; now we wanted to take a closer look at their red kangaroos, their emus and, if we were lucky, some of the ancient fossils embedded in their rocks.

We crossed salt-streaked wastes of crimson where only small whirlwinds of sand, known in the Outback as willy-willys, danced in the emptiness; and then flew past Lake Torrens, the salt lake that blocked the explorer Edward Eyre's route to the interior in 1840. It glittered pink in the sun, as if the last rich, red dyes of the Centre were draining into puddles on this margin of the arid zone. We flew on over tawny earth squeezed into rounded hills with acacias wriggling along the dry watercourses that encircled their bases. Soon the hills grew sharp and tall, thrown into stark relief by the vivid afternoon light.

This landscape was vastly different from the monolithic outcrops of Ayers Rock and the Olgas that we had left behind. We crossed wild, jagged country the colour of worn, yellow velvet, tufted with the green of native pines, and with only a pink flush left in the soil. Below us rose the main crest of the Flinders, in some places sliced into fearsome angles of bare rock, in others smoothed into hard, rounded stumps—testaments to the awesome geological upheavals of the past.

The Flinders' tallest peak reaches only 3,900 feet, but the ranges carry a rich weight of the earth's history. In Pre-Cambrian times, a great trough fed by ocean waters extended far into the continent. For a thousand million years rivers flowing from the landmasses on either side discharged their sediments into the trough, causing continual subsidence. An ice age followed and glaciers scoured the land, dumping their ballast of rock fragments into the trough and building up an estimated 1,500 feet of coarse glacial sediment on top of the mud and sand deposited by the rivers. When the ice melted, running water laid down further deposits so that the sediments accumulated on the sinking sea-floor eventually reached a total thickness of several miles.

The process continued into the early Cambrian period, when primitive invertebrates first appeared. But about 500 million years ago the subsidence ceased. Geological pressures caused the sediments to buckle and fold, forcing them up into a long mountain chain, and the water was pushed southwards. The newly formed ranges were gradually levelled away by the elements. Seventy million years ago, however, more geological convulsions thrust up the stumps of the

The erosive force of water has left its imprint on the low ground skirting Bunker Hill in the Flinders Ranges. Thick, clay sediments, carried from higher ground by sheets of run-off water, have been worn by streams into a maze of gullies whose walls are being further eroded into ridges and runnels.

earlier highlands, creating the present Flinders Ranges. Erosion has carried away most of the fossil-bearing limestone of Cambrian times, so that the greater part of the Flinders is composed of older and more resistant rock strata in which no traces of elemental life have been found. But there are still sections of Cambrian limestone in the ranges and some of these, I knew, were filled with tiny fossilized skeletons of life-forms that once flourished on the Cambrian sea-floor. Perhaps we should find our own haul before leaving the Flinders.

For the moment, however, there were other things to think about. Landing our aeroplane was one of them. According to the map, there was an airstrip just beyond Wilpena Pound, an immense natural amphitheatre set into the Northern Flinders, and so-named by 19th-Century settlers who were struck by its resemblance to a pound or stock enclosure. We flew low over the landscape and soon the unmistakable features we were searching for came into view. Below us was a colossal oval saucer studded with gums and native pines, and hemmed in by ramparts and rugged peaks of red-brown sandstone. The floor of the Pound is seven miles long and three miles wide across the middle, and is drained by a creek that has cut a gorge more than a mile wide through the north-eastern wall of the enclosure.

There has been much speculation about the Pound's origins. According to one Aboriginal legend, its walls were formed by two mighty serpents that died, head to head and tail to tail. Another legend tells how a monster, known as Kaddi-Kra, was driven to seek refuge underground and was trapped beneath a great pile of earth and rock. The rumbling sounds caused by occasional earth tremors in the Flinders are said to be the frantic subterranean scrabblings of Kaddi-Kra seeking to escape.

Travellers and early settlers believed the Pound was the filled-in crater of a vast and extinct volcano. A likelier explanation was advanced by A. R. C. Selwyn, the geologist who surveyed the Flinders in 1859 for the government of South Australia. "The Pound", he wrote, "is not a volcanic crater, nor in any way due to volcanic action but simply to an undulation of the sandstones that form the summits of all the higher peaks from Mount Remarkable northwards."

We circled, looking for the little-used 3,000-foot airstrip that has been scraped out from an expanse of yellow spear grass and lies close to the gorge. We missed the strip on the first circuit, but the second time around I spotted it. As we landed and rolled bumpily to a halt, the little aircraft quivering like a butterfly, half-a-dozen red kangaroos that had been disturbed by the noise of the engine bounded past with exultant grace and were soon lost from sight in the sea of enveloping grass.

Climbing stiffly out, we stretched our limbs, luxuriating after the long flight, and then gathered round the map. We planned to make for the headquarters of the Flinders Ranges National Park, which is at Oraparinna, a former grazing property some 20 miles north-east of Wilpena Pound. Although hardly the brightest jewel in the 140,000-acre park, Oraparinna is conveniently situated for excursions into some of the wilder parts of the Flinders and so we had arranged to use it as our base for the next few days.

We left the aeroplane where it stood and set off to look for a near-by homestead that was marked on the map, trusting that here we could obtain transport to Oraparinna. For about a mile we waded through the chest-high yellow grass and then crunched along the blue shale-bed of a dried-out creek, watched by pink-breasted galahs gathered like blossoms in the great, river red gums on the banks. A lone emu fled before us, teetering wildly on elongated legs as it disappeared round a bend in the creek.

After another mile or so, we reached the homestead and were readily provided with refreshment and a lift to Oraparinna. On the way we drove through former grazing land that is returning to its wilderness state. Some of the wounds inflicted by livestock and cultivation, however, were still depressingly apparent. Settlers spread from the south to this region in the 1880s, first bringing sheep and later clearing the native saltbush to plant wheat. The wheat shrivelled and died during droughts, and the farmers left in 1914, penniless. But the damage to the land had been done. Stripped of vegetation and with no roots to bind it, the soil was whipped away by the wind or carried off by floods. Further ravages have been inflicted by the herds of feral goats that wander the area, scratching for vegetation on the hills.

The denuded landscape compared poorly with what we had seen of Wilpena Pound. The Pound has also suffered the same pattern of grazing, cultivation, drought and flood. But in 1920 it was made a forest reserve and the richness of the soil and an average rainfall slightly higher than that of surrounding areas have restored its grandeur.

Arriving at Oraparinna, we met Herman Bakker, chief ranger of the Flinders Ranges National Park, and were accomodated in a guest-house that had once been sheep shearers' quarters. Herman's knowledge of the Ranges proved to be rivalled only by his enthusiasm, and thus infected we woke early next morning anxious to begin our first excursion. We were joined by two of Herman's friends, King and May Fisher, who had driven south from their cottage at Blinman 15 miles away. May is an Australian potter who was lured to the ranges by the startling colours of the clays—purple, red, green, yellow and pink; King, an American, is a jazz musician. Both proved to be excellent guides to the Flinders.

King also seemed to specialize in comic encounters with animals. We had driven in Herman's Land Rover towards Mount Sunderland, a few miles south-west of Oraparinna, and parked beneath its sand-gullied stone slopes. King was leading us in a scramble over a rockslide when we looked up to see a big, red kangaroo poised about 30 yards ahead of him. The 'roo was a thick-chested five-footer with immense muscular development. King and the 'roo both froze, regarding each other closely, while we stood back to watch what happened. King took the initiative, essaying a few slow hops towards the beast, his pack bouncing on his back. The 'roo raised its head in polite, cautious acknowledgement and took a few matching hops forward. Then it was King's turn, then the 'roo's, then King's again, and then the 'roo's—each performing the grave measures of their incongruous minuet until, eventually, a dry creek-bed blocked any further advance. Then the 'roo turned about, as if to say, "Well, I'll be saying g'day to you now," and sailed elegantly away.

I had seen kangaroos in other parts of the Centre, but had never got so close to a red kangaroo, the largest of more than 90 related species. Unlike the grey kangaroos, which are restricted to wet habitats, the reds

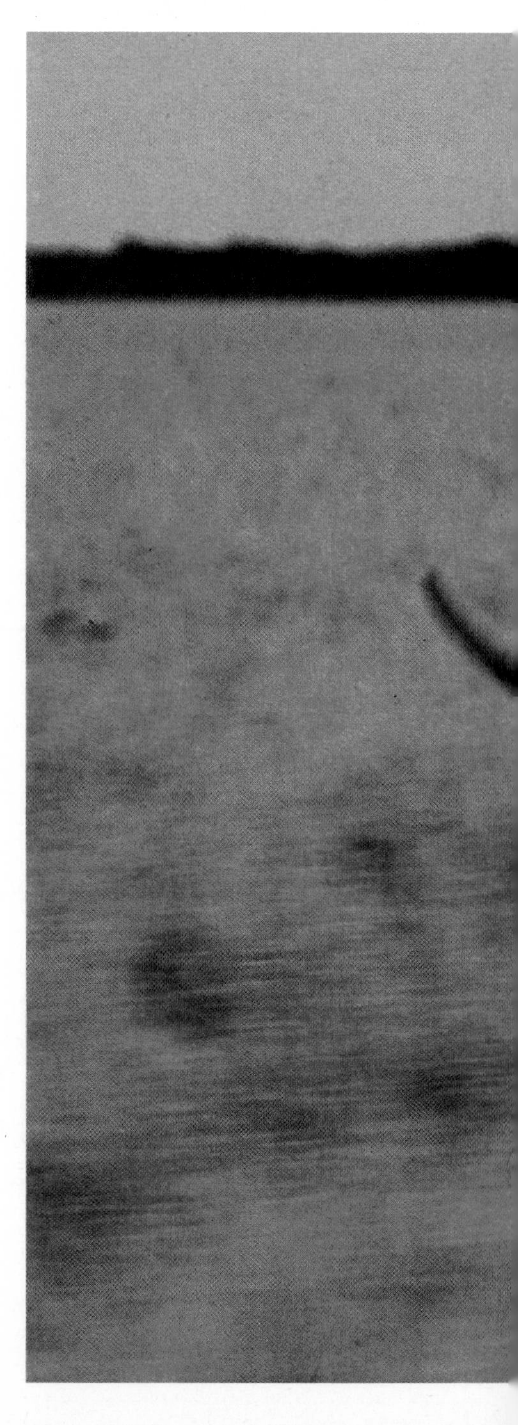

A male red kangaroo bounds over a grassy plain at 30 miles an hour, holding its rudder-like tail stiffly behind to help maintain balance.

range over a million square miles of Australia, including most of the arid Centre. Their essential requirements are short green grass for feeding, some shade where they can retreat at the height of the day, and drinking water—and being desert animals they can survive on remarkably little of the latter. Those we saw in the Flinders seemed to live in fairly small social groups of not more than ten animals. Like many other Outback creatures they are nomadic rather than migratory, following variable food supplies. Sometimes a well-grassed area in a good season will attract hundreds of 'roos, although such large aggregations are rare.

Because of its strength, a full-grown red has few natural enemies, but dingoes kill them when they attack as a group. Although well able to take care of themselves, red kangaroos are usually shy creatures. Whenever we flushed them from their shady retreats under trees they raced off through the grass at speeds up to 30 miles per hour, making 30-foot leaps with their hind legs and using their thick tails as rudders. But they can keep up this kind of pace only over short distances, and as soon as the 'roos felt they were out of danger, they dropped on to all fours, taking modest, seven-foot strides.

Like all marsupials, the young kangaroos—called joeys—are born only partly formed and complete their development in their mother's pouch. It is a fascinating business. The new-born 'roo is about an inch long and weighs less than an ounce. Its eyes and ears are barely formed; and with only a sense of smell to guide it and strong fore-paws to climb with, the baby makes the immense journey from vagina to pouch, usually unaided by its mother. Once there, it fastens itself securely on a teat, and remains in the pouch for six months, until it is big and strong enough to risk short journeys outside. For several months after that, however, the joey will return to the pouch—so long as the mother has no objections. On one occasion I saw a yearling 'roo that must have weighed all of 50 pounds wrestling with its mother in a vain attempt to return to its early security.

An emu, one of the largest flightless birds, paces across a plain in the Flinders Ranges. Adult emus, which stand up to five feet high, have few natural enemies. Emu chicks, however, take 18 months to reach full size and are meanwhile vulnerable to attacks from birds of prey and dingoes. For this reason they spend the growing period under the care of their fathers.

The late Sir Hans Heysen, the Australian painter whose canvases convey so much of the atmosphere of the Flinders, once wrote of the "spell" the ranges cast over him, describing each of his trips to the area as "an exhilarating experience in form and colour". It was not difficult to understand what he meant. The Flinders look impressive from the air; from the ground I found their impact overwhelming. Around us, the peaks and ridges rose like brick-red battlements against a hard blue sky, while sun and shadow gave distant rock masses a purple luminosity. Summer days are long in the ranges, but for us time passed all too quickly and, with the sun sinking low in the sky, we climbed aboard Herman's Land Rover and headed back to Oraparinna.

As we bumped over scrub and plain, we heard about another of King's comic encounters with the Flinders wildlife. The Fishers were staying in a ramshackle hut in a lonely part of the ranges. One morning May was in the hut baking bread and King sat sketching on the bank of a near-by creek-bed. Suddenly, May heard her husband give a strange, strangulated cry that sounded like: "I-don't-want-to-make-a-noise-but-for-Pete's-sake-come-outside-and-have-a-look." She emerged to find King with two emus in attendance.

King had been so absorbed with his drawing that it was some time before he became aware of his two onlookers—strange, ungainly-looking birds whose massive, long-plumed bodies and broad-beaked heads gave them the appearance of something between an ostrich and a pterodactyl. One of them stepped away along the creek-bed as soon as May appeared, but the other remained gawking over King's shoulder, scrutinising his sketch of the scene. Cocking its head to one side, it withdrew awkwardly and then rubber-necked over King's other shoulder. The bird was not tame, simply consumed with curiosity. But having satisfied its curiosity, it made off, flapping its wings in a kind of flying run. In spite of its clumsy appearance, the emu is amazingly fast when it has to be, reaching speeds of up to 40 miles an hour.

The Flinders have been a stronghold of emus for thousands of years and the Aborigines believe that the red ochre deposits found in parts of the ranges are the blood stains of a mythical giant emu killed by dingoes. Tribesmen used to walk hundreds of miles from the north to collect this ochre for ceremonial and magical rites. Aboriginal dances feature exaggerated movements based on the emu's gait, and deep in the Flinders Ranges representations of the birds appear in rock carvings estimated to be more than 3,000 years old.

The tribesmen prized the emus for their flesh and eggs. They also used the birds' leg sinews to bind spearheads to shafts and they stuck emu feathers together with human blood to make the dreadful *Kurdaitja* shoes. These foot coverings were worn by medicine-men and by avengers of crimes in the Centre—men who padded relentlessly through the desert on the trail of their intended victims. The Aborigines used to catch emus by exploiting their insatiable curiosity, encouraging them to approach by waving bunches of feathers over rocks and bushes. The birds were then netted or corralled behind brush fences. Sometimes, the

Aborigines employed less subtle tactics, lighting fires around waterholes and tossing stones at the birds to confuse them and force them into the water where they could be easily dispatched. Among the missiles were tektites—rocks of meteoric origin believed to be the eyes of ancestral emus and also said to possess magical powers of control over all living birds.

Like the red kangaroo, the emu is nomadic, moving about in small groups in search of the grass on which it mainly feeds. Its long legs enable it to cover great distances, and at harvest-time crowds of them materialize from the Outback deserts to congregate on wheatfields, trampling and eating the crop. The emu's gluttonous appetite and its habit of stampeding through paddock fences at top speed make the bird a scourge of farmers, who shoot it and smash its eggs whenever they can. In 1932 the authorities in Western Australia were even persuaded to send a detachment of Royal Australian Artillery on a mission to wipe out 20,000 emus that were threatening a local wheat harvest. The mission, however, was not a success; the emus simply scattered and, after a couple of months' skirmishing, the army returned to barracks.

Tramping along dried creek-beds or scrambling over the flushed face of the ranges, we saw emus and kangaroos in plenty. But the fossils I had hoped to find proved more elusive, and it was not until the day before we were due to leave the Outback and fly back to Sydney that we had success. Awakened early by shrieking flocks of little corellas settling in a stand of river red gums near our quarters at Oraparinna, we breakfasted with Herman Bakker and then set off with him in the Land Rover for Brachina Gorge, where he knew there was a fossil-bed. The gorge forms an outlet at the western end of the Aroona Valley, a wonderfully fertile oasis set between two flanks of the ABC Range. The valley is irrigated by Brachina Creek, which flows for 24 miles, descending into the gorge as Lubra Springs.

We drove through mallee scrub, habitat for the mallee fowl, a hen-sized bird that hatches its eggs in an "incubator" of warm, rotting vegetation. Red-capped robins trilled in the scrub and above us flew flocks of seagulls going to join the tens of thousands of other waterfowl on the brief, wet miracle of Lake Eyre, 200 miles to the north. Herman steered us expertly through the spinifex, startling euros that had been lying in squats in the centre of the tussocks. We also disturbed an Australian pipit that suddenly fluttered across our path, feigning injury to distract our attention from her nest.

A bullock track used by teamsters in the last century leads through

A Centrally-heated Nest

The mallee fowl of southern Australia hatches its eggs in a remarkable way. The female lays her eggs in an "incubator", which the male builds by filling a hole with vegetation; the vegetation ferments and produces heat to warm the eggs.

Regulating the temperature of the incubator is left to the male. He does this by probing the mound with his heat-sensitive tongue, testing for the vital 92° F. required for successful incubation. According to the "reading" obtained, he adjusts the temperature by scraping on or raking off soil (right) to trap or release heat.

Each egg takes eight weeks to hatch, and because there may be 35, laid at weekly intervals, neither parent has time to care for the young. But the chicks are independent from the moment they hatch; they dig their own way out of the mound and can fly within a day.

A MALLEE CHICK EMERGES FROM ITS NEST.

A MALE MALLEE FOWL REGULATES THE TEMPERATURE OF ITS EGG MOUND BY SCRAPING AWAY THE SOIL ON TOP.

the valley and beyond Brachina Gorge, but after a few miles we decided to park the Land Rover and continue the journey on foot. We followed the winding creek, lulled by the sound of slate fragments clinking musically against the green, algae-draped rocks on its bed. Flood-scarred gum trees lined its banks and on the gentle hills above grew bushy, lime-green acacias. In places there sprouted clumps of Sturt's desert pea, the most striking of all Outback plants. Its long, blood-red and black flowers, growing in clusters of six and eight on short stems, glistened like waxen pagodas against a background of soft, grey foliage. Beside them, the violet, bell-shaped flowers of the emu-bush blazed amid lemon-scented grass.

"Aroona" is said to be a native word for running water and, although there are no lakes in the valley, the creek has formed many pools among the lichen-encrusted rocks scattered close to its course. We saw grey teal and white-faced tern swimming in the clear water and a colony of fairy martins hunted insects over the creek, returning with their prey to the bottle-shaped nests they had built beneath the overhanging banks. I also caught a glimpse of a rare yellow-footed rock-wallaby leaping up a fault-line in a rock face, its barred tail and neatly striped body giving the impression of ceremonial regalia.

We reached Brachina Gorge at last and filed between its high sandstone walls, listening to the cicadas that rasped like tiny electric motors in the gum trees around Lubra Springs. Deep in the gorge we came to a tumble of mauve limestone boulders, dotted with the dung of euros that had come to drink from the springs. As we were straggling past the boulders, Herman stopped suddenly, scooped water over them and then stood back like a magician about to unveil his most spectacular trick. The moistened rocks darkened and I saw that they were crammed with fossils—so many that they seemed to make up most of the stone. Impressed in the boulders were the medallions of antiquity: scores of the tiny skeletons of *Archaeocyatha*. The Greek name for these long-extinct marine organisms means "ancient cup" and derives from their cup-shaped outer and inner shells, the walls of which were joined by delicate radial spokes. The shells were riddled with holes through which sea-water would have circulated.

About 500 million years old, *Archaeocyatha* are among the earliest fossils yet found—and among the most puzzling. Some paleontologists believe they were primitive corals, some think they were sponges, and some that they were early species of seaweed. The most widely accepted view, however, is that they were the ancestral stock from which both sponges and corals derived, and they have been tentatively assigned to a class by themselves: the Pleospongia.

While the others walked on down the gorge in search of more fossils. I remained by the mauve boulders pondering on my Outback journey. The Centre can be hard and cruel, a drear and killing wasteland. But it also has a harsh and undeniable beauty that is found nowhere else. I recalled some lines from an Australian writer, Ray Ericksen, who abandoned university administration and foreign travel to follow the tracks of Ernest Giles. "It was variety," wrote Ericksen, "that I wanted to see again: the wide-ranging eucalyptus and acacias, the hakeas and grevilleas, the host of related and unrelated trees and shrubs and wildflowers that clothe this continent. I missed the hard forms, the contorted branches and the peeling bark; and I missed the colour, the great range of muddy greens, the fiery reds and the laughing yellows. I missed the unpredictability of it all: the smell of eucalyptus oil drawn off in vapour by the sun, the scent of boronia heavy in the evening air. I missed the sounds: twigs and leaves swish-rattling along the ground before the blast of a hot northerly. I wanted a hard light again and a genuinely blue sky."

Ericksen seemed to sum up all the diverse attractions that the Centre held for me. The heart of Australia, which so many travellers described as dead, beats powerfully. I realized that from the ancient fossils embedded in the boulders beside me to the kangaroos and emus roaming the inland plains stretched an unbroken chain of life. There were times I would never forget: sweltering beside that tiny, hot pool at Dalhousie Springs where I had searched for the desert hardyhead; or climbing over the ridges of the Simpson Desert and seeing my first truly wild dingo; my first view of Ayers Rock and the Olgas, and the wildflowers blooming on the plain that surrounded those myth-shrouded monoliths; my journey into the mysterious, shadowy gorges of the Macdonnell Ranges. We left the Outback the following day. As we winged across the Flinders on the long flight back to Sydney, I knew that one day I would return. I had not suffered the desperate privations and shattered hopes of so many of the 19th-Century explorers; but, like them, I was now held tightly in the Outback's embrace.

A Metamorphic Rock

Viewed from afar, Ayers Rock looks like an impregnable fortress built in some bygone age by a mythical warlord. Rising more than a thousand feet out of the inland plain 200 miles south-west of Alice Springs, the mammoth outcropping has deep-rooted walls scarred and pitted as though by a thousand sieges. But while the massive bulk of the Rock appears immutable and infinitely durable, the constancy of its colours is as fleeting as time itself.

As each hour passes, the surface of the Rock mirrors the changes of the unfolding day (overleaf). Each variation of light, shade and weather projects a different colour on the monolith. On a clear day, the transitions are as gradual as the sun's movement through the sky: too slow to be noticed by an onlooker. But when each extreme of colour is recorded by the camera, Ayers Rock seems to have a life of its own.

In the first light of morning, the Rock is suffused with a rusty flush. Later, as the sun climbs towards its zenith, the monolith appears bleached of colour and is flooded with a light so brilliant and direct that its gullies and crevices are illuminated, making it appear flat and two-dimensional. When clouds trail across the sun, the hot-hued surface deepens to a richer brown, with the sharp pink of its feldspar layers eclipsed by the duller tones of sandstone. After rain, Ayers Rock turns a leaden colour, and green clumps of spinifex spring up around it. Now it looks cooler and less threatening, a distant castle that might offer shelter to a wanderer lost in the surrounding expanse.

Evening provides the most spectacular colour change. When the sun sinks low, its rays transform Ayers Rock into a gargantuan ember. Outlined against the wan blue heaven, the incandescent Rock seems to scorch the sand for miles around.

Viewed from above, Ayers Rock assumes a different shape and character, its curves accentuated by the parallel gullies that striate its summit. Its mass appears dissipated, with the hard line of its profile no longer silhouetted against the sky. In the dim light of dawn or dusk, shadows deepen in the cavernous bays that rim the Rock, and each crack and fissure is thrown into bold relief. It is easy then to imagine Ayers Rock as a ruined temple roofed with a carved and rutted dome, and guarded by gloomy portals cut deep in its sandstone walls.

AYERS ROCK RISES OUT OF THE EMPTY PLAINS

CLOUDS TURN AYERS ROCK A RICH BROWN

IN SHADE THE ROCK TURNS SOMBRE

AYERS ROCK PALES IN THE MIDDAY SUN

AT SUNSET IT ASSUMES A RUDDY GLOW

EVENING SHADOWS ACCENTUATE THE ROCK'S GLOOMY PORTALS

Bibliography

Baglin, Douglas and Mullins, Barbara, *Australian Wildflowers in Colour*. Angus and Robertson, 1968.

Bonython, C. W., *Walking the Flinders Ranges*. Rigby, 1974.

Breeden, Stanley and Slater, Peter, *Birds of Australia*. Angus and Robertson, 1968.

Calvert, Albert F., *The Exploration of Australia, From 1844 to 1896*. George Philip and Son, 1896.

Carter, Jeff, *A Guide to Central Australia*. Sun Books, 1972.

Carter, Jeff, *Outback in Focus*. Angus and Robertson, 1968.

Carter, Teho, *In a Strange Land: Pioneers of Australia*. Dennis Dobson, 1964.

Chippendale, T. M., *Wildflowers of Central Australia*. Jacaranda Press, 1968.

Chisholm, A. H. and Serventy, Vincent, *John Gould's The Birds of Australia*. Lansdowne Press, 1973.

Clune, F., *Dig*. Angus and Robertson, 1971.

Corbett, L., and Newsome, A., *Dingo Society and its Maintenance, A Preliminary Analysis In*: Fox, M. W. (ed.) *The Wild Canids*, Van Nostrand Reinhold, 1975.

Davey, Keith, *Australian Desert Life*. Periwinkle Books, 1969.

Dutton, G., *Australia's Last Explorer: Ernest Giles*. Rigby, 1974.

Fitzpatrick, Kathleen, *Australian Explorers, A Selection from Their Writings*. Oxford University Press, 1958.

Frauca, H., *Animal Behaviour*. Periwinkle Books, 1971.

Harney, W., *To Ayers Rock and Beyond*. Rigby, 1971.

Harney, W., *Tales of the Aborigines*. Rigby, 1974.

Hodgson, Margaret and Paine, Roland, *A Field Guide to Australian Wildflowers*. Rigby, 1974.

Hooper, P. T., Sallaway, M. M., Latz, P. K., Maconochie, J. R., Hyde, K. W. and Corbett, L. K., *Ayers Rock-Mt. Olga National Park Environmental Study, 1972*. Land Conservation Series No. 2. Australian Government Publishing Service, 1973.

Hudson, Lionel, *Dingoes Don't Bark*. Rigby, 1974.

Immelmann, Klaus, *Australian Finches in Bush and Aviary*. Angus and Robertson, 1965.

Innes, Hammond, *Australia*. Andre Deutsch, 1971.

Joy, William, *The Explorers*. Angus and Robertson, 1974.

Knowles, Peter, *Australia's Wild Heart*. Rigby, 1974.

Laseron, Charles Francis, *Ancient Australia*. Angus and Robertson, 1964.

Laseron, Charles Francis, *The Face of Australia*. Angus and Robertson, 1972.

Lockwood, D., and Roberts, A., *Northern Territory Sketchbook*. Rigby, 1968.

Madigan, C. T., *Crossing the Dead Heart*. Rigby, 1946.

Marlow, Basil, *Marsupials of Australia*. The Jacaranda Press, 1962.

McGregor, Craig, and Beal, David, *Life in Australia*. Southern Cross International, 1968.

Mincham, Hans, *The Story of the Flinders Ranges*. Angus and Robertson, 1964.

Mincham, Hans, *Vanished Giants of Australia*. Rigby, 1966.

Morcombe, Michael, *Australia's National Parks*. Lansdowne Press, 1969.

Morcombe, Michael, *Australia's Wildflowers*. Lansdowne Press, 1970.

Morcombe, Michael, *An Illustrated Encyclopaedia of Australian Wildlife*. Macmillan, 1974.

Mountford, Charles, *Brown Men and Red Sand*. Phoenix House, 1950.

Mountford, Charles P., *Ayers Rock, Its People, Their Beliefs and Their Art*. Angus and Robertson, 1965.

Newsome, A. E., Corbett, L. K., Best, L. W. and Green, B., *The Dingo*. Australian Meat Committee Review No. 14, 1973.

Ride, W. D. L., *Native Mammals of Australia*. Oxford University Press, 1970.

Rolls, Eric C., *They All Ran Wild*. Angus and Robertson, 1969.

Serventy, Vincent, *Landforms of Australia*. Angus and Robertson, 1968.

Slater, Peter, *A Field Guide to Australian Birds, 2 Vols*. Scottish Academic Press, 1970.

Smith, Robin and Willey, Keith, *The Red Centre, The Landscape and People of Outback Australia*. Frederick Muller, 1975.

Spencer, Baldwin (Editor), *Report on the Work of the Horn Scientific Expedition to Central Australia, 2 Vols*. Dalau and Co., 1896.

Stone, C. R., *Australian Landforms*. Angus and Robertson, 1968.

Stuart, John McDougall, *Explorations in Australia: The Journals of John McDouall Stuart—1858, 1859, 1860, 1861 and 1862*. Saunders, Otley and Co., 1864.

Tillyard, R. J., *The Insects of Australia and New Zealand*. Angus and Robertson, 1926.

Walton, K., *The Arid Zones*. Hutchinson University Library, 1969.

Worrell, Eric, *Reptiles of Australia*. Angus and Robertson, 1963.

Acknowledgements

The author and editors of this book wish to thank the following: Tony Allan, London; Dr. N. Arnold, British Museum of Natural History, London; Herman Bakker, Ranger-in-charge, Flinders Ranges National Park, South Australia; Dr. D. Blaxell, Royal Botanical Gardens and Herbarium, New South Wales; Dr. J. Bowler, London; Ian Cawood, The Northern Territory Reserves Board, Alice Springs; Fiona Clyne, London; H. G. Cogger, The Australian Museum, Sydney; Charles Dettmer, Thames Ditton, Surrey; Aleen Hanley, Wildlife Preservation Society of Australia, Sydney; Sally Heathcote, British Museum of Natural History, London; Richard Hills, London; Richard Humble, Devon; Jim Hicks, London; Norman Kolpas, London; Alan Lothian, London; C. McCarthy, British Museum of Natural History, London; Rob McTavish, London; Russell Miller, London; Mike Newth, Glamorganshire; Heather Sherlock, Ashwell, Hertfordshire; Dave Simpson, London; The Staff of Australia House Library, London; M. J. Tyler. The University of Adelaide, South Australia; Dr. A. Warren, University College London; The Zoological Society of London.

Picture Credits

Sources for the pictures in this book are shown below. Credits for the pictures from left to right are separated by commas; from top to bottom they are separated by dashes.

COVER—Phyll Bennett from Natural Science Photos, London. Front end papers 1, 2—Richard Woldendorp. Front end paper 3, page 1—R. J. Griffith. 2, 3—G. R. Roberts. 4, 5—Graham Pizzey from Natural History Photographic Agency, Westerham, Kent. 6, 7—Robert B. Goodman. 8, 9—Phyll Bennett from Natural Science Photos. 14, 15—Map by Hunting Surveys Ltd., London. 18—G. R. Roberts. 20—A. G. Wells from Natural History Photographic Agency. 23—Dr. J. M. Bowler. 25—Isobel Bennett from Natural Science Photos. 31—Robin Smith. 32—Robert B. Goodman. 33—Robin Smith. 34, 35—John Cavanagh. 36—G. R. Roberts. 37 to 39—Isobel Bennett from Natural Science Photos. 40, 41—David Moore from The Photographic Library of Australia, Sydney. 44, 45—to be advised. 49—Douglass Baglin. 51 and 55—Hans and Judy Beste. 56—K. H. Switak from Natural History Photographic Agency. 57—Graham Cowles. 58—Bruce Coleman Ltd., London. 59—Douglass Baglin from Natural History Photographic Agency. 60, 61—Robin Smith. 65—J. P. Ferrero from Ardea, London. 67 and 71—Laurie Corbett. 72—J. P. Ferrero from Ardea. 77—Paul Green-Armytage. 78—Rennie Ellis from Scoopix, Melbourne. 79—Robin Smith. 80, 81—Paul Green-Armytage. 82—Joe Jennings. 83—R. J. Griffith. 84, 85—Paul Green-Armytage. 89—G. R. Roberts. 91—R. J. Griffith. 93—Eric Lindgren from Ardea. 94—G. R. Roberts. 99 to 101—R. J. Griffith. 102—Robin Smith. 103—Graham Cowles. 104—Hal Missingham. 105—Graham Cowles. 106, 107—Robin Smith. 111—Paul Green-Armytage. 114—Robin Smith. 117—C. A. Walker from Natural Science Photos. 119—Graeme Chapman from Ardea. 124 to 135—J. Roger Hayne. 139—Mary Evans Picture Library, London. 141—Map by Hunting Surveys Ltd. 144, 148 and 151—Mary Evans Picture Library. 155 to 161—*Horn Scientific Expedition to Central Australia*, 1896. Eileen Tweedy by courtesy of the Committee of the London Library. 164—Phyll Bennett from Natural Science Photos. 167—Graham Pizzey from Bruce Coleman Ltd. 168—Dr. D. R. Harris from Robert Harding Associates, London. 170, 171—Graham Pizzey from Bruce Coleman Ltd. 175—J. Roger Hayne. 176—Robin Smith–Jonathan MacQuitty. 177—Rennie Ellis from Scoopix. 178, 179—David Moore from The Photographic Library of Australia.

Index

Figures in italics refer to illustrations.

Colour reproduction by Irwin Photography Ltd., at their Leeds PDI Scanner Studio.
Filmsetting by C. E. Dawkins (Typesetters) Ltd., London, SE1 1UN.
Printed and bound in Italy by Arnoldo Mondadori, Verona.